GUIDE TO DIESEL MARINE ENGINES

JOHN FLEMING

Editor: Ellen Harden

Bristol Fashion Publications
Harrisburg, Pennsylvania

Complete Guide To Diesel Marine Engines, by John Fleming

Published by Bristol Fashion Publications

ISBN: 1-892216-24-8
LCCN: 00-133159

Contribution acknowledgments

Inside Graphics: By the author or as noted
Cover Design: John P. Kaufman
Cover Photo: Detroit Diesel

DEDICATION

I dedicate this book to my father, the late John M. Fleming, Sr. He held a Chief Engineer's License for ocean going vessels and it was he who told me the stories that fired my imagination and turned my world into a sphere inhabited by combustion engines. Those stories were exciting tales of big ships and the mighty diesel engines that drove them.

As a lad of eleven my father fell overboard from a boat several miles off the Carolina Coast and drifted for three days without a life jacket, supported only by his own determination. He finally swam ashore and was eventually returned to his Augusta, Georgia home, to attend his own funeral. I still have the newspaper clippings.

The other John Fleming was an adventurer who rode the Mexican border with the old Fifth Georgia Cavalry. Eventually he became the last Commander of the Last Man's Club for that storied group they called the "Richmond Hussar's."

His army days came before I was born and the man whom I remember seldom spoke of wars or strife. Instead he brought to life the world below steel decks where iron men fought every kind of adversity to keep those huge engines turning. I will always remember those tales.

INTRODUCTION

The diesel engine is surrounded by a certain mystery that conjures up visions of massive motors with the ability to move mountains. The fertile mind of German engineer, Rudolph Diesel is generally conceded to be the origin of the four-stroke diesel engine in common use today. The engine was initially a rather clumsy and primitive product as were most other types of engines we have produced, in their early incarnations. The first venture Herr Diesel made into the realm of internal combustion engines ended with an explosion that tore the engine apart and nearly ended the life of the gifted inventor.

The diesel is an internal combustion engine and it runs on a controlled explosion. That explosion is very real and it must truly be controlled. The second engine was an operating success. It was built and run in 1897. The diesel has performed well, ever since.

The four-stroke diesel has evolved over the years and spread out to almost every area of utilization. Less common but still very important as a modern day power source is the two-stroke diesel. Invention of this engine is generally credited to an Englishman named Dugald Clark.

The work of Dugald Clark won him a knighthood and he eventually became Sir Dugald Clark. The two-stroke diesel also found easy acceptance into the world of big engines and heavy loads. In this country the General Motors Corporation embraced the two-stroke diesel with open arms and Detroit Diesel was the result.

There are many kinds of diesel engines that power our locomotives, submarines, towboats, and other heavy-duty vessels. There is also a new generation of high speed, high performance diesel engines that run in sport fishermen and faster yachts.

As long as twenty years ago a Cummins four-stroke diesel actually ran in a racer at Indianapolis. It was so successful it was ruled out of competition. That Cummins had the potential to run the entire race without a refuel and at record speeds.

Diesel engines have run at Bonneville on the Great Salt Lake where sheer, blinding, speed is the only god and men risk life and limb for that last fraction of a mile per hour. I accept this and I enjoy it at some level for I am a racer at heart but this is not the view of the diesel engine that I grew up with.

The first diesel engine that I ever worked on was a 100 horsepower Atlas. This 100 horsepower engine weighed about 4,000 pounds. It turned 165 maximum RPMs and was still running in the same harbor tug after 35,000 hours. It looked as big as a house to me. In fact, it was as big as the voluminous engine room that contained it. I stood in awe and stared at that huge engine. The flywheel was as tall as I was and it had a ponderous power that seemed literally unstoppable. That was an honest hundred horsepower from a serious engine. I will always remember the smell. Diesel fuel from the engine, juniper from the planking, saltwater from the sea, and perhaps a bit of sweat from those who labored over that trusty power plant. All combined in one exotic fragrance I will never forget.

Wherever men go down to the sea in real wooden ships that smell is to be found and it is never to be forgotten. As I grow older I sometimes walk aboard a modern fiberglass yacht and find myself waiting for that smell to come, but it never does.

You cannot turn back the clock on the march of time and indeed, why try? Modern engines are lighter, faster and in many cases, stronger. You have only to listen to the high pitched scream of a turbo charger turning over 150,000 RPMs to know something special is going on inside the engine.

Electronics have added their special twist to the new age of diesel power and as you read, you will learn what contributions to diesel operation have resulted from the marvel of electronic controls.

Within these pages I will provide a detailed view of the construction, operation, and fascination of the diesel engine. I hope you will find the material within these pages to be both instructive and entertaining.

John Fleming

TABLE OF CONTENTS

CHAPTER ONE
MYTH & MYSTIQUE

I want to use this first chapter to discuss the abilities and the limitations of the diesel engine. I will explore the mystique of this special power plant and add a few myths. The diesel has been called many things.

It is an oil engine because it runs on fuel oil. It is also a heat engine because it uses heat to ignite the fuel oil. The diesel is a compression ignition engine because it uses compression to generate heat which ignites the fuel in the cylinder. It is an internal combustion engine because it burns fuel oil inside the cylinder of the engine. The diesel engine is many things but there are also some things, which it is not.

The diesel is an endurance engine, good for many hours of service but with limitations.

The diesel is designed to do a number of things very well but there are some things that it does not like to do. The diesel is not a start and stop engine. Frequent starts and stops are bad news for any diesel and the engine will wear disproportionately during start up and shut down. Steady RPMs and continuous operation are the forte of this engine.

Given the conditions of steady, reasonable operating speeds and continuous duty, the diesel engine may literally run for years without shutdown or service. Installed as a power source for electric generators for instance and running on a constant filtration system for the lubricating oil, the diesel will run indefinitely.

In this type of service, day in and day out, without a whimper, the diesel engines will tote the load. Under some conditions it may not last so long.

At the other end of the spectrum, there is a new breed of diesel designed to compete in the high performance boat arena. This engine is like a candle that burns brightly for but a moment, and is then extinguished. It does a great job but for a much shorter time.

Thus the diesel engine has many faces, so do not form judgments about exactly what it is, or is not, until you have finished this book.

Figure 1

This 1948 Clark Diesel engine turns 400 maximum RPMs.

A diesel may develop more torque than a gasoline engine of comparable horsepower, though this is not an absolute. It may not develop more torque than a gasoline engine of comparable cubic inches. This assumption is based upon the premise that both power plants are naturally aspirated.

The reasons for this verity are seated in the design and mechanics of internal combustion engines as a whole. In fact there are several mechanical principles involved in the torque/horsepower comparison between the diesel and the gasoline engine. I will describe each of these in detail for you as we progress.

It is odd to believe a diesel has more horsepower than a gasoline engine but many do believe.

Dr. Einstein gave us the Atomic Interval chart and in doing so took us out of the science of absolutes and introduced us to the science of comparisons. Instead of saying oxygen is light today we say oxygen weighs 16.

Instead of saying lead is heavy, today we can say lead weighs 200.59. These are exact descriptions with an understandable meaning. It was important to get these numbers accurate and it is important to get the horsepower ratings of our engines described accurately so we may know what to expect of a given engine.

One horsepower is an exact measurement. It is equal to 33,000 lbs./ft. of work, per minute and it makes no difference whether the source is gasoline or diesel. If the engines are disparate, one from the other, then the horsepower is also disparate. A dozen is 12 items, more than that is not a dozen. A foot is 12 inches, more than that is not a foot.

Respect the horsepower for what it is, a unit of measure. Expect the manufacturers to do the same. Advertising should be accurate and factually based. So long as the advertised horsepower is accurately measured for each engine, there will be no difference between gasoline engines and diesel engines.

If there is to be a new rule or a new measurement that rule or measurement should be advertised and made known. But until such time as this is done, the scientific value of one horsepower is not different between gasoline engines and diesel engines.

DON'T BELIEVE THE DIESEL IS OFTEN OVER RATED

The diesel engine may have any one of several horsepower ratings and it generally conforms rather closely to that particular rating, whichever one is chosen. A Continuous

Horsepower or Continuous Duty Rating and an Intermittent Horsepower or Intermittent Duty Rating are two of these choices.

The continuous horsepower rating is the amount of horsepower the engine can produce on a steady basis without over working the engine. It is the equivalent of the cruising speed of a gasoline engine. Operating at or slightly below this level, the diesel engine is quite happy.

The intermittent horsepower rating is the amount of horsepower the engine can produce for short spurts, a few minutes at a time. This is the full throttle rating of the engine and it is generally higher than the continuous horsepower rating. In some cases it is much higher.

At this speed the life of the engine will be much shorter.

There may also be a Yacht Rating, which is always based upon maximum output. To achieve this rating the engine may require special injectors, increased Rpm's and other modifications. The yacht rating is for light duty and it is not to be confused with what the engine can do on a day to day basis.

Advertisements often emphasize the intermittent, full speed, or yacht rating, ratings of the engine and often do not print the continuous duty ratings. Though that information is readily available, the failure of some advertisers to circulate the information may lead to the perception that the engine you bought was over rated.

Always ask for the continuous duty rating of any engine you intend to buy. You need this information even if you intend to run the engine hard at all times. The difference between continuous duty and intermittent duty ratings is not great on some engines but much greater on others. With this information in hand, you can better decide how much you are willing to give up in order to hurry up.

The diesel is a heavy duty, slow speed engine, but not always.

There are many slow speed, heavy duty diesel engines in use today, but the really startling development in diesel engines is the high speed, light weight, engine that powers our sport fishermen and faster yachts.

Roger Penske, Stewart and Stevenson, and Johnson and Tower are three of the sources for high speed, high performance diesels. How much performance? In the heyday of fast cars and mega engines we looked at one horsepower per cubic inch as a measuring device. The 427 cubic inch Chevrolet at 425 horsepower is an example.

A rarity was the 327 cubic inch engine, also from Chevrolet, that developed 375 horsepower. That has never been done, before or since. No one has produced a stock, factory production engine that made 1.15 horsepower per cubic inch in a domestic automobile.

I am presently working on a 6-V53 Detroit diesel that has 6 cylinders with 53 cubic inches of displacement for a total of 318 cubic inches. It has dual turbo chargers feeding into a supercharger and both systems pumping boost to the engine. This diesel engine produces 425 horsepower from just 318 cubic inches and that is about 1.34 horsepower per cubic inch.

Not what you would expect from a diesel but exciting, nonetheless. How far will this trend go? Who knows? We are in a new Century and the new ideas just keep coming.

I will tell you about these diminutive power house engines as well as the heavies.

THE DIESEL ENGINE MAY HAVE A LONG STROKE

In the '40's and even into the '50's the diesel engine had the long stroke, small bore configuration and the length of that stroke was the source of its high torque output. Very slow speed engines are still built in that under square configuration but many of the newer, high-speed diesels are not.

The newer Ford 7.4-liter diesel engines and the GM 6.2-liter diesel engines are prime examples of high-speed diesels with an over square configuration. In this system the bore is larger than the stroke. The short stroke diesel is a fact of life today but it is also a fact that this type of engine has sort of slipped up on the average boater.

We closely observe the outside of the diesel engine, the paint, the logo, and the graphics. The mundane and the ordinary are there to be seen but we seldom consider the internals and even if we do, the implications are often lost on us. I will try to remedy that also.

GASOLINE IS DANGEROUS BUT SO IS DIESEL FUEL

One of the very real differences between gasoline and diesel engines is the fuel they burn. The gasoline fuels are much more volatile than is diesel fuel. Gasoline has a lower flash point; thus it is more likely to cause an engine room fire than is diesel fuel. Fires at sea are scary indeed and this alone causes many mariners to choose diesel power.

However the fact that diesel fuel is less likely to explode does not mean it will not explode. Under the proper conditions diesel fuel will blow your boat away. Never forget it. Fumes from diesel fuel are lighter and more volatile than the fuel itself and they can be very dangerous.

DIESEL DOES NOT HAVE MORE POWER THAN GASOLINE

Diesel fuel has about 19,550 BTUs of heat energy, per gallon while gasoline has about 21,400 BTUs of heat energy, per gallon. The advantage, by about 1,850 BTUs per gallon, goes to gasoline. There is about 0.095 percent more heat energy in a gallon of gasoline than in a gallon of diesel fuel.

This nine plus percent difference in the fuels contributes a number of interesting characteristics to the diesel/gasoline engine comparison. Those comparisons will become a part of this text. There are other properties of the two fuels that decidedly favor diesel fuels. Remember gasoline is an abrasive.

DIESELS DO NOT NATURALLY SMOKE

Environmentally friendly diesels with electronic fuel injection are becoming quite common on both the highways and the waterways of our country. These engines burn only the needed amount of fuel and make precious little smoke, if any.

How they achieve this remarkable performance is an interesting story in itself. Low emission diesels are a tribute to the ingenuity of those who build them. As you read this book, I will give you a close look at how they do it.

FUEL CONVERSION

Every machine must have a purpose and the diesel engine is no different. It is designed to make usable power from a chemical fuel and the manner in which it does this can be described in a short form as well as in great detail. Let us begin with the short form.

The diesel engine takes a chemical fuel and converts it to heat energy by burning. It then takes the expanding gasses and converts them to reciprocating motion, back and forth or up and down. Next, it converts the reciprocating motion to rotating motion, around and around.

Now we have energy in a form we can utilize to do work. This is a simple description and of course a more detailed approach is needed. For this purpose we should consider the parts of the engine, the movements and the events that accomplish these results.

CHAPTER TWO
PARTS OF THE DIESEL

In this chapter I am going to provide you with a short description of the parts of a typical diesel engine. I will give each part a name so we understand what we are talking about as each part is referred to through out this book.

Begin with the engine block. The skeleton on which the engine is built. A diesel may have the cylinders cast In Bloc, In Pairs, or Individually. Cylinders cast in bloc have a single casting for the entire group of cylinders. Cylinders cast in pairs have two cylinders cast together.

Cylinders cast individually feature single cylinders standing upon a common base. The value of a system that employs cylinders mounted individually or in pair' lies in the economy of repair.

Onto this cylinder block we bolt a cylinder head. The cylinder head covers the top of the cylinder and supports the valves, rocker arms, fuel injectors, and in some instances, the camshaft.

The engine employs a crankshaft that has an arm to which we will apply pressure and in turn generate torque. The crankshaft has journals on which the crankshaft and connecting rods turn. It has counter weights, which are lobes cast or forged onto the crankshaft with centers 180 degrees away from the rod journals.

The engine uses a piston that accepts pressure from the burning diesel fuel and delivers that pressure downward. Piston rings seal the sides of the piston so the heated gasses will remain under control and will not escape the cylinder. A wrist pin connects the piston to the connecting rod.

A connecting rod connects the pistons and the crankshaft, each to the other. It has an "I" beam construction. It has provisions for bearings or bushings at the wrist pin or little end and at the connecting rod or big end. The connecting rod and its bearings take considerable punishment.

Figure 2

This connecting rod from a heavy duty diesel weighs slightly less than an entire 350 cu. in. Chevrolet marine engine.

The engine employs a camshaft that operates the valves and lets air into the engine or exhaust gasses out of the engine. The camshaft may operate some accessories on the engine. The camshaft is a critical part of the engine and it's design influences performance of the engine.

The diesel uses a lubricating oil pump to furnish lubricating oil to the various parts of the engine, under pressure. Diesel oil pumps deliver high volumes of lubricating oil. The oil itself is an important part of the engine cooling process.

A primary fuel pump provides fuel to the injector pump. The primary pump creates low pressure but the injector pump raises this pressure much higher. Injector pumps may be any one of several types and I intend to explore these in detail later.

A timing gear or timing chain attaches the crankshaft to the camshaft and drives the camshaft. Whether a timing gear or timing chain is employed, either device has a surprising load to carry. The camshaft has a number of springs bearing down directly upon its lobes.

The flywheel of the diesel engine carries the engine through from stroke to stroke. The diesel flywheel tends to be quite heavy and the slower the engine turns, the greater is the need for weight in the flywheel. Flywheels are very interesting guys.

The diesel engine employs a number of bearing shells at various points such as rod and main journals. These shells are half circles, steel shells with bearing metal cast onto the surfaces. We call them insert bearings because the shells are inserted into the rods or mains.

A crankcase or pan is bolted to the base of the block. This pan holds the lubricating oil and closes the lower end of the engine block. Housed within this pan and bolted to the engine block is the lubricating oil pump. The lubricating oil pump provides lubricating oil to the critical parts of the engine.

Some diesel engines are raw water-cooled. They are

directly cooled by seawater but these engines are in the minority. Most diesel engines are heat exchanger cooled or have closed circuit cooling. The engine is simply too expensive to be exposed to the ravages of saltwater.

The diesel engine may be naturally aspirated, supercharged, or turbo charged. The naturally aspirated engine uses no mechanical booster to feed air to the engine. The supercharged engine uses a mechanically driven blower to force feed air into the cylinders. The turbo charged engine uses a blower driven by exhaust gasses to force feed air into the cylinders.

The engine must have a raw water pump to provide cooling water (seawater), either directly to the engine or in the case of closed circuit cooling, to the cooling unit. The engine must also have a circulating pump that helps to circulate coolant throughout the system.

A diesel engine starter motor can be either electrically powered or driven by compressed air. This is a bit of an aside but there are a few diesel engines that employ donkey motors to start the diesel. The donkey motor is a small gasoline powered unit that turns the diesel until it gets heat in the cylinders. These are seldom seen on boats but they are an interesting part of heavy equipment engines and worth you knowing about. There are so many variations involved in diesel construction and just as many interesting stories about each of these differences.

Alternators provide current to charge the batteries that start the engines and they are described as totally enclosed and explosion proof when employed on a marine engine. The manufacturers of these devices are eminently aware that diesel fumes can be dangerous.

The diesel engine may be equipped with a glow plug. The glow plug is a heater that warms the cylinder of the engine before starting. There are other devices for this purpose. They are largely a feature of older engines and I will discuss them in the chapters on heavy-duty power plants.

In the next chapter I will begin to put the flesh of

greater detail on the bones of these early descriptions. The beginning chapters of this book may seem tedious but I urge you to read them and think about each part as you read. In the beginning I want to build understanding but as the book progresses I will certainly take the reader as far into the world of diesel as a primer can go.

CHAPTER THREE
THE ENGINE & CYLINDER BLOCK

In general and for the purpose of this treatise, consider those engines that produce full horsepower at speeds from 1,800 Rpm's to 4,000 Rpm's to be light duty engines. Those engines which produce full power at speeds around 1,000 Rpm's are ordinarily medium duty engines. Heavy-duty engines will produce full power at speeds from 150 Rpm's to about 500 Rpm's.

All of these engines share a commonality of parts and function but those parts may look a bit different from engine to engine. Before we have finished we will thoroughly explore all of those similarities and each of those differences. Let us first address the matter of light to medium duty engines.

The diesel engine is built on a foundation, which we call an engine block. This designation is somewhat different for the diesel than for the gasoline engine because the cylinder blocks may be cast separately from the engine block. The basic engine block may only be a kind of base which houses the crankshaft.

The cylinder block may be cast singly or in pairs. They are then bolted onto the top of the engine block and can be removed in similar fashion. The advantage to this system lies in the ability to repair any one of these individual cylinders without tearing down the entire engine. Should the engine coolant freeze at some time it is entirely possible that only one or two of these cylinders would be effected.

The engine block may be cast of aluminum but it is generally manufactured of cast iron. The block has one or more bores which house the pistons and those bores may be in any one of several configurations. The configuration of the bores determines our description of the block. It may be a "V" block or an in-line block and unlike the gasoline engine, it may have just about any number of cylinders.

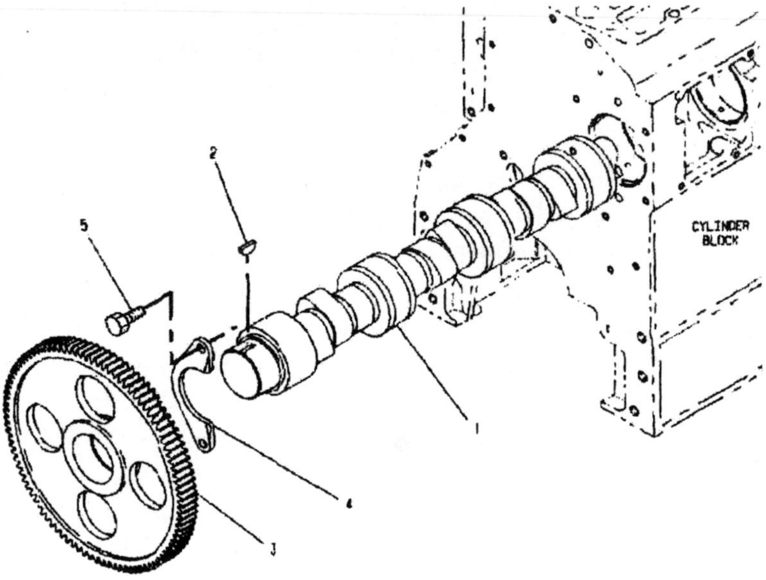

Figure 3

The open bores, deck, water and oil passages, push rod holes and many other portions of the block can be seen in this illustration.

The light duty or medium duty diesel engine will have an enclosed crankcase. The crankcase will have a pan that encloses the lower parts of the engine and holds the lubricating oil supply. The lubricating oil pump is mounted inside this pan and fitted with a king of sieve or open wire filter to prevent debris from entering the pump.

On heavy-duty diesel engines the lower end of the engine may be open and these engines are referred to as A frame or open crankcase engines. I will devote a chapter to the matter of these heavy-duty engines at a later time. For now we will stick to the smaller framed diesel.

Looking at the naked cylinder block, from the top view, we can see the number of cylinder bores and the webbing or deck that constitutes the top of the block. The block may or may not be fitted a sleeve or liner. If a sleeve is fitted, that sleeve is a replaceable steel cylinder liner pressed into the block.

The engine, which has no such liner, is often referred to by old time diesel mechanics as a throwaway block but this is an unfair criticism. The unlined block can either be bored out to an oversized piston or bored out to the dimensions at which a liner can be installed. In fact, that unlined or sleeveless block offers both options as a choice for the rebuilder.

A sleeved block may use a dry sleeve or a wet sleeve in its cylinders. The dry sleeve is pressed into a block with solid cylinder walls and simply lines that fully formed cylinder. The sleeve is very thin, generally less than .060 (sixty, one thousandths of an inch). The sleeve is dry because no coolant touches it.

The wet sleeve is pressed into a block with an open area below the deck. The wet sleeve is much thicker than the dry sleeve because it stands alone, supported by the block at top and bottom only. The wet sleeve must be quite stout since only the walls of the sleeve retain the pressure of combustion. It is considered to be a wet sleeve because the coolant is directly exposed to its outside surface. There are seals at top and bottom to keep water from entering the cylinder and to keep compression or burned gasses out of the water jacket. The installation of these cylinder seals is critical to the performance of the engine.

The use of either dry or wet sleeves makes the engine rebuildable many times and the life of the engine almost limitless. The diesel engine is quite expensive. A small sailboat auxiliary can be purchased for about $4,000 dollars. Even these small engines cost nearly as much as a 260 horsepower gasoline engine. A 1,000 horsepower diesel has a cost measured in cubic dollars and its larger cousins may cause the banker to check his vaults before committing to a loan for the money to buy a new one. Thus it is very important to be able to rebuild and extend the life of the diesel engine.

The diesel engine block has a set of saddles or supports for the main bearings cast into the bottom of the block. Braces called, webbings support those saddles and make them more rigid. The main bearings on the diesel operate under very heavy loads.

Rifle drilled passages inside the block are combined into a gallery from which lubricating oil is distributed to critical points. The gallery delivers oil to the top of the block to lubricate parts on the cylinder heads. It also delivers lubricating oil to the main bearings. The connecting rods get their lubricating oil indirectly from the mains.

There are holes in the crankshaft and the crankshaft itself is hollow. These holes accept lubricating oil from the main bearings and deliver it through the hollow crankshaft, to the connecting rod journals. There is no detectable loss of pressure and the system is quite satisfactory.

The cylinder block will have a set of scantlings cast into the structure. Scantlings are simply a thickening of the block on these smaller engines and they add strength to certain areas that are subject to greater stress.

There are machined surfaces at several points on the cylinder block. The top and bottom of the block for the attachment of head and pan, the front and rear of the block for seals and gaskets, and the main bearing saddles. The machine work on the main bearings is quite critical. All alignment of the moving parts of the engine is derived from the mains. The bearings must be in perfect alignment if the crankshaft is to run easily in the bearings. To this purpose, the block is align bored with a single boring bar run through each of the bearings, in turn. The line established through the main bearings is the axis to which all other critical machine work is indexed.

The top of the cylinder block is indexed to this line so the cylinder tops will all be an even distance from the centerline of the crankshaft. The cylinder bores are concentric (truly aligned) to the connecting rod journals because they too are aligned to the crankshaft index.

The main caps are the bottom-half of those bearing saddles which are located at the base of the block. These caps will often have four or more bolts to retain them in place and they are made from heavy castings. All the pressure exerted on the crankshaft by the fuel burning in the cylinders is focused on the main caps.

The pressure from above is trying to drive the crankshaft through the bottom of the crankcase and the main caps are the only restraint that prevents this. The bolts that hold the main bearing caps in place are high tensile-strength steel. Usually about 225,000 pounds/inch square (grade nine) is a good estimate for these bolts.

The sides of the diesel engine block may have inspection plates so the rod bearings can be inspected upon removal of the cover this allows the engine to be rebuilt in frame. All the parts save the main bearings and the crankshaft can be replaced during an in frame overhaul.

This is an overview of the engine block/cylinder block and their relationship. Now let us move on to the cylinder head.

CHAPTER FOUR
CYLINDER HEADS

The cylinder head of a diesel engine is a rigid casting and it must accept high pressures while sealing the gasses of combustion inside the cylinder. The cylinder head may be designed for only a single cylinder, when the cylinders are cast individually, or it may be designed for a pair of cylinders, if they are cast in pairs. Surely the cylinder head may also be built as a cover for all the cylinders in any cylinder bank as well, provided the cylinders are cast in bloc. The separate nature of these parts allows for a bit of individual movement among those parts and this is one of the few objections to the use of this method.

Cylinder heads for gasoline engines have the combustion chambers cast or machined into their inner areas. Cylinder heads for diesel engines may have combustion chambers located in the head but this is often not the case. There are many diesel cylinder heads that are completely flat on the inside portion towards the cylinder.

In this situation the combustion chamber is cast or machined into the piston itself. A piston with the combustion chamber cast into its crown or top may have a bit of space between the piston crown and the deck of the cylinder block when the engine is at top dead center. This space adds to the combustion chamber volume.

Diesel engines may have a pre-combustion chamber cast into the head. This is a small, roughly tear drop shaped, chamber into which the injector sprays fuel. The first combustion occurs here and burning gasses are delivered to the whole cylinder from this chamber.

The pre-combustion chamber allows the use of lean mixtures in the diesel and it is believed to help with flame propagation. Flame propagation is a phenomenon I will devote a later chapter. It is a truly fascinating study.

The cylinder head may have only a single valve or it may have as many as four valves for each cylinder. These valves may be either intake valves which inlet air or exhaust valves that emit burned gasses. In some engines there may be only exhaust valves provided. The reasons for this difference will become apparent as we discuss four-cycle diesels versus two cycle diesels and their comparative operation.

Figure 4

The head has ports for air, water, oil, etc. Mounting attachments for the head, rocker arms and injectors are also machined into the head.

The valves for a diesel engine may have hard seats installed. These seats are made of stellite or a similar hard metal with a high tolerance for temperature. The cylinder head is broached or machined to accept these seats and they are pressed into the hole created by the broaching tool.

This is much different from the gasoline engine that is sometimes advertised as having hardened valve seats. On the gasoline engine the hardening is done through an electrical process called induction hardening which effects only a few thousandths of the surface metal.

The cost is lower but the valve wears through this hardened area rather quickly. The first valve grind will surely remove this hardened metal if wear has not already done so. Induction hardening is neither so effective nor so long-lived as the installation of hard seats.

The cylinder head has ports for the intake of air and the release of exhaust gasses. These ports are passages through the cylinder head that enter or exit the cylinder. They are cast into the head during manufacture. There is a class of diesel that uses only exhaust ports and has no intake ports in the head. This is a special type of engine and it will also be discussed during the two-cycle/four-cycle comparison. Now I want to stay with four-cycle diesels and their operation.

There are water passages cast into the diesel cylinder head. They run across the tops of the combustion chambers and behind the valve pockets. Of course these same passages carry coolant other than water in a closed circuit cooling system.

The rocker stands or rocker studs support the rocker arms atop the cylinder head. These fixtures carry the rocker arms themselves and permit the change of direction in the force generated by the camshaft. The camshaft exerts upward force and the rocker arms turn this into downward force to activate the valves.

There are passages for lubricating oil drilled into the heads themselves. They may have additional tubing for distribution of lubricating oil affixed to the head. Other holes in the cylinder head align with holes in the block to receive coolant from the block, into the head.

A gasket between the head and block seals the surfaces and it too has holes which permit the flow of lubricating oil or coolant. A very few diesel engines use gasketless cylinder heads. These engines depend upon closely machined surfaces and high tension torquing of the head bolts to effect a seal. There are few of these engines about.

A few diesel engines with finned, air cooled, cylinder heads and cylinders have been built but they were almost universally unsuccessful. The engines ran hot in closed engine rooms and they were doomed to a short life. A few years ago I worked on one of these engines but the performance was dismal.

There are holes drilled into the outer walls of the cylinder head which have stamped metal freeze plugs installed. These holes are drilled at strategic locations and provided in the hope the soft plug will push out and the head will be spared if the coolant should freeze. In actual operation this is generally a wasted effort. When coolant in the head freezes the plugs usually push out as intended but the cylinder head is usually cracked anyway. The idea is great in theory but perhaps a bit less impressive in its performance.

Cylinder heads for the diesel may be attached to the cylinder block with stud bolts or cap screws, depending upon the designer's convictions. For whatever style of bolt or screw employed, there must be very little stretch in the fastenings.

The high pressures and unique vibration frequencies of the diesel engine exert tremendous strain on these guys. If they stretch, just a little bit, or walk around even slightly, the gasket will leak.

We have those stationary parts, the block and head behind us. Now let us begin with things that go around and around.

CHAPTER FIVE
THE ROTATING ASSEMBLY

The rotating assembly consists of the crankshaft, the flywheel, the harmonic balancer, the lower portion of the connecting rods, and the drive plate or drive gear for the transmission. In a word, all of those things which go around and around.

I have listed the connecting rods (big end) in this chapter on the rotating assembly and you will find them listed again in the next chapter (little ends) on the reciprocating assembly. The reason for this will be explained in a complete discussion on balance.

The crankshaft is the major element of the rotating assembly but it is certainly not the only element. Each part of the rotating assembly must work together and in harmony if the engine is to perform well. We will consider all of the parts of the rotating assembly in this chapter but let us begin with the central figure in this group, the crankshaft.

The diesel crankshaft may be constructed of cast iron, nodular iron, or steel. The cast iron or nodular iron shafts are actually cast in a foundry using a sand mold. The steel crankshaft is usually forged. Forging is a hammering process that tightens and compacts the molecules in the structure of the forging and toughens the metal.

The crankshaft then goes to the machine shop to have the journals and other parts of the crankshaft finished. The general process of machine work is much the same for either the cast iron or forged steel crankshafts. The general features of any crankshaft are roughly alike. Let us consider these features in detail.

The crankshaft has a series of journals. They are designated as crankshaft journals and connecting rod journals. The crankshaft journals are the central structure the crankshaft rides upon. They are at the centerline of the crankshaft and are supported by the main bearings.

There is an arm that extends away from the center of the crankshaft and ends at the connecting rod journal. This connecting rod journal supports the big end of the connecting rod and receives pressure from that connecting rod to operate the engine.

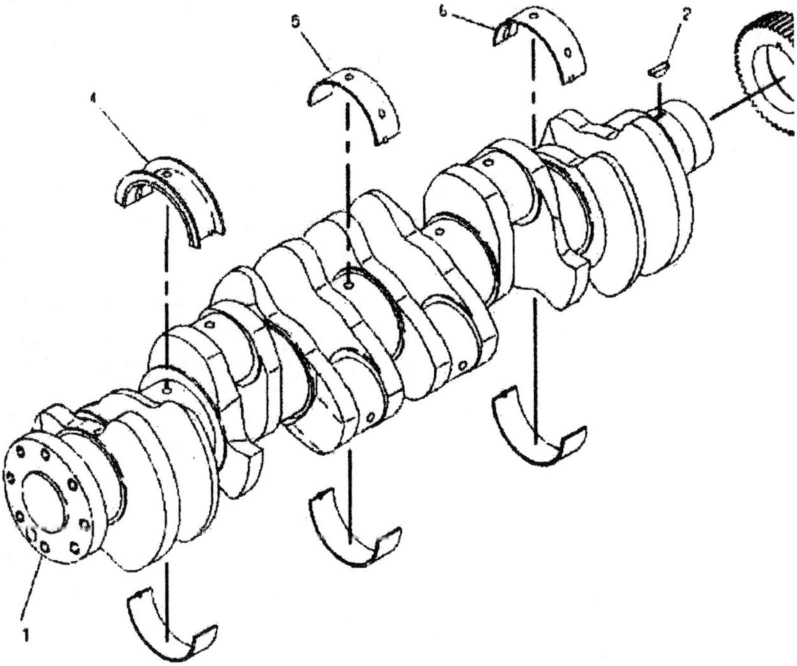

Figure 5

The crankshaft with all it's cast and machined parts.

If we measure the distance from the centerline of the main bearing journal to the centerline of the rod journal, this is half the length of the stroke. Stated in another way, "Multiply the distance from the centerline of the main bearing journal to the centerline of the connecting rod journal by two and the result will be the length of the engine's stroke."

The in-line engine generally has one main bearing journal for each cylinder, plus a front and rear journal at each end of the crankshaft. This results in five main journals for a four-cylinder engine or seven main journals for a six-cylinder engine.

The opposed piston engine has a crankshaft with a main bearing arrangement similar to the in-line engine but the "V" bank engines are different. The V bank engines have a single main journal for each two cylinders, plus a front and rear main. There will be five mains for each eight-cylinder engine.

On an in-line engine or an opposed piston engine, the crankshaft will also have one set of rod journals for each cylinder. On the engine with a V configuration there is generally one rod journal for each two cylinders. In this system, two connecting rods share a common main bearing journal. This sharing of a connecting rod journal is the reason for the difference in the number of main bearings per cylinder found between the engine configurations. If you were really interested in how this situation lays out it would be instructive to go to a diesel shop and observe the different crankshafts.

The crankshaft will have one or more counterweights. The centerline of these counterweights will be located 180 degrees away from the centerline of the connecting rod journal. Thus the weight is located in a position, which is exactly counter to the weight of the connecting rod journal, and anything attached to it.

The counterweight is usually semicircular in nature but the centerline and center of balance for the counterweight are still directly away from the centerline of the rod journal. The counterweight may be fully machined or it may be left as cast with a rough finish. The choice of finish tells us a bit about how serious the manufacturer is in his pursuit of quality.

The crankshaft must be strong and yet it must have the ability to flex to some degree. It must be hard enough to resist the wear of the bearings but it must not be so hard as to become brittle. The simple matter of selecting a metal for the crankshaft is not simple at all.

The crankshaft has a flywheel attached to one end. The flywheel and its weight are valued for the inertia force it generates. Inertia is the tendency of a body in motion to remain in motion, until acted upon by a greater force. The flywheel uses the inertia force created by its movement to carry the engine through from stroke to stroke.

The flywheel is important on a gasoline engine but it is a vital part of the operation of the diesel. The diesel engine develops a great deal of compression pressure, which offers substantial resistance to the rise of the piston in the cylinder. After the piston passes through top dead center and begins to fall, any pressure on the top of the piston helps it on its way. Before the piston reaches top dead center however, any pressure on the piston top is trying to push the entire rotating assembly backwards. The diesel engine often rotates very slowly at idle speed and the inertia in that flywheel may be the only reason the engine runs.

There are two general types of flywheels that depend on the theory of balance employed by the designer. Some flywheels are for internally balanced crankshafts and in this system the flywheel is but a weight. It supports the starter ring and provides inertial force to the crankshaft. Other flywheels are for externally balanced engines. In this system the flywheel still provides inertial force to the crankshaft and serves as a support for the starter ring as well. Yet it also provides another function. The flywheel has a special weighted area cast or machined into its body that is a part of the balancing system for the engine. I will expand on this when we balance the engine but for now I only want to make you aware of its existence. One thing that you must remember however is this, "Never confuse an externally balanced flywheel with an internally balanced flywheel, even though they bolt right up to the same crankshaft." There have been instances when engine manufacturers changed from one system to the other on the same or similar engines and the flywheels had like bolt patterns. If you miss match the flywheel and the crankshaft the result will be sudden and disastrous. The engine will literally shake itself to pieces.

The drive plate is bolted to the flywheel. It transmits power from the engine to the transmission and it must be considered in any balance system as an integral part of the crankshaft/flywheel because it is fastened to the rotating assembly.

Many diesels do not drive from the flywheel end but rather employ an additional gear on the crankshaft at the timing gear end to drive the transmission. These gears are of comparatively small diameter. They are fully machined and they have no need for balancing.

Crankshafts with gear driven outputs to the transmission generally have externally balanced flywheels. The reason for this is obvious in light of the fact that there is nowhere to mount a conventional harmonic balancer.

The harmonic balancer rotates with the crankshaft and it is located outside the timing gear cover at the timing gear end of the engine. The term harmonic balancer may be a bit of a misnomer. The term is widely used but, in fact, the device itself does not actually balance the engine. The harmonic balancer generates a vibration of its own. The frequency and amplitude are such that we do not perceive its existence. It serves the purpose of breaking up the stronger vibrations that occur from other causes within the engine. I will put the matter of balance into better perspective shortly.

Some of this material will be repeated during the chapter on balance. I hope I can be forgiven for this lapse since the parts of the engine and the various functions thereof are truly inseparable, each being a part of the whole.

Crankshafts deserve your close attention and I hope you will consider everything you read about them. Learn the names of the parts and the function of each. Then as we continue to add parts to the engine you will be able to see each of them in turn and understand what they do.

CHAPTER SIX
RECIPROCATING ASSEMBLY

The reciprocating assembly consists of all of those things that go up and down or back and forth. The parts of the reciprocating assembly are the piston, piston rings, wrist pin, wrist pin locks and the little end of the connecting rod.

The pistons for a diesel engine are generally made of aluminum, although a number of larger engines will have cast iron pistons. The piston serves the same purpose as that of a gasoline engine. It accepts the pressure generated within the cylinder of the engine and delivers that pressure to the crankshaft, via the connecting rod.

The piston has a crown or face, which is the top of the piston. This top may have a regular shape or it may be indented for the combustion chamber. The sides or skirts of the piston extend below the piston ring grooves.

The piston rings ride in a set of lands and grooves machined into the side of the piston. The groove is the internal portion and the land is the external portion of this area. The land is the portion above the groove. These grooves are fitted very closely to the shape of the piston rings to prevent leakage around their perimeter.

Diesel pistons are very expensive indeed. On larger engines it is possible to re-machine the ring grooves and install a spacer to tighten the rings in the grooves and reseal them against leakage. This used to be a common practice in bygone years when labor was cheaper. At that time the re-grooved piston was common on even smaller engines but today it is seldom seen. It is not a practice you are likely to run into unless you are working on heavy duty, slow speed engines or doing a bit of restoration.

The skirts are longer on the diesel piston than on the gasoline engine. This added length to the skirt provides additional stability in the cylinder bore but of course it will also create a bit more drag. This drag is considered acceptable for the sake of longevity.

Figure 6

The diesel engine piston is a great deal different from a gasoline piston. Note the piston rings located above and below the wrist pin.

The piston skirt is cam ground. Cam grinding produces

an oval shape represented by an alphabetical designation. They will appear as an "A" cam, "B" cam, etc. The letter indicates the degree of flatness in the sides of the oval. The flatter sides of this oval are located on the same part of the piston as the wrist pin boss.

The wrist pin boss is a thickened area in the piston that carries the wrist pin bores. These bores are the holes into which the wrist pins are installed. Thc wrist pins may be installed into these bores with a press fit or there may be bearings.

A press fit is one in which the wrist pin is approximately .0005 or five-ten thousandths of an inch larger than the hole. This makes the pin fit tightly indeed and requires the piston be heated to accept the wrist pin or a considerable amount of pressure applied.

The wrist pin also passes through the little end of the rod. This is the manner in which the piston is connected to the connecting rod. There may be a bearing in the top portion of the little end of thc connecting rod. This presents us with three possibilities.

First there can be a bearing in the wrist pin boss with the wrist pin tight in thc rod. Second, there can be a bearing in the little end of the connecting rod with the wrist pin press fit into the piston. The third possibility assumes a full floating wrist pin. In this scenario the wrist pin has a bearing surface at both the wrist pin boss and the little end of the connecting rod. It literally floats freely at all points and, of course, this is the most friction free situation possible for the wrist pin.

The wrist pin locks are generally made of strong wire in the shape of a 3/4 circle. Alternatively, they may appear as patented Circ Clips that require special pliers to remove. The Circ Clip has a flat surface with broadened ends. Holes are drilled in those ends for the extended tips of the special pliers that remove and install them.

Pistons for the diesel engine resemble those for the gasoline engine in many ways. The general shape and overall construction are similar but after that has been said, the similarities begin to blur. The diesel engine uses a much heavier piston, even for the same bore diameter, than does the gasoline engine. The diesel piston is subjected to much higher pressures and in the case of the turbo charged diesel, higher temperatures. The diesel often runs in detonation at low speeds and the engine must accept this added pressure. Then also, the diesel piston often extends upward above the wrist pin boss to a greater degree than does the gasoline piston. This is because the diesel piston often has the combustion chamber in the piston top. The combustion chamber is machined into the crown and the injector sprays fuel directly into this indentation. Heat and pressure generated by combustion requires a great deal of integrity in this area of the piston assembly.

The connecting rod for a diesel engine is generally longer and thence must be stronger than that of a gasoline engine. There are several reasons for this. First, the diesel engine develops very high cylinder pressures and the long rod has more leverage against it, thus it must be stronger.

Why so long? There are several reasons. First, the diesel engine generally has a longer stroke than does its gasoline counterpart. That is not always true as we will see in later chapters but it is a good rule of thumb for diesel construction. The longer stroke requires a longer connecting rod so the piston skirt can clear the crankshaft counter weights.

Then there is the matter of rod angularity, which has a considerable effect upon developed torque. The longer rod generates more torque for a given pressure on the piston tops. We will also explore this phenomenon at a later time.

The diesel engine usually employs a split cap connecting rod. It may have only two retainer bolts to hold the caps onto the rods, just as the gasoline engine uses but it may have several. Large engines sometimes employ four or more connecting rod bolts to hold the caps in place.

The rod may be rifle drilled along its length. This produces a passage through which oil is delivered, under pressure, to the top bushing in the connecting rod. In past years many of the higher priced automobile engines used this system. Packard and Rolls Royce both employed this approach in the '40's and later.

There are some connecting rods on larger diesel engines which have holes in the small end of the rod to spray oil onto the under side of the piston dome. This is for cooling purposes and the oil is also applied to the piston skirts for the same purpose. This is a very effective way to cool the internal parts of a large engine.

Connecting rod bearings for the diesel are generally tri-metal bearings constructed in much the same manner as those designed for use in the gasoline engine. They employ three different metal layerings over a steel shell or backing but here the similarity ends again. Bearings for the diesel engine are much harder than those employed in gasoline engines. They must be hard enough to prevent the bearing metal from being displaced under high stress and pressure. The harder bearing is very effective and it lasts well but it imposes some restrictions upon the engine builder.

Hard bearings are very unforgiving of your errors and they demand you build a clean engine. The softer bearings employed in gasoline engines generally have good embedding qualities and this serves to save the engine from the effects of foreign objects in the lubricant.

Small stray particles in the crankcase are absorbed into the surface of the softer bearings on the gasoline engine and their negative effects are partially or totally neutralized. Those harder bearings on the diesel are totally unforgiving and any particles that passes into the bearings are likely to cause extensive damage to the bearing, the crankshaft, or both.

The engine builder must carefully clean all surfaces of the diesel engine and pay particular attention to the internal passages, the oil gallery and the other areas where oil is carried. Diesel engines are expensive and the parts reflect this fact. Longevity for a diesel engine depends upon careful attention to detail.

I realize every person who has any experience in engine rebuild or overhaul is thinking, "What the heck, you gotta keep all of 'em clean." That is a very good and healthy attitude but listen up, "If you are not accustomed to building diesel engines, when you begin to do so, add a healthy dose of scrubbing to the process."

We now have an understanding of the reciprocating assembly and the rotating assembly. In the next chapter we will join the two and see if we can get it to balance. Balance and imbalance represent success and consequence. If the engine is balanced it will be successful but if it is not, the consequences may be drastic, even terminal for the diesel engine.

CHAPTER SEVEN
BALANCING THE ENGINE

We often speak of balancing the internal parts of an engine. Few mariners, indeed few mechanics, actually understand balance in the engine or what is required to attain that balance. In fact, balance alone is only half of the process involved.

There are all sorts of forces generated by the moving parts of the diesel and they are continually flying around inside that cast iron cubicle we call the engine. How we manage to control those forces is an interesting proposition.

The effort generally consists of two parts. Balance is the first of these parts while counter balance is the second. The reason for this dual approach lies in the nature of the engine and the parts thereof. As discussed in earlier chapters, there are two different types of moving parts in the engine, rotating parts and reciprocating parts. We can balance the rotating parts of the engine, those parts that go around and around. We cannot balance the reciprocating parts, those parts that go back and forth or up and down. The reciprocating parts can only be counter balanced. The two balancing processes become an interesting exercise in practice, for each process requires an "Even application of forces."

The one group of forces moves around a particular center, the centerline or axis of the crankshaft. The other group of forces moves up and down, to and from the axis of the crankshaft. To understand the principals involved you must also understand the physical operation of force in a straight line and force in a rotating element.

Let us look a bit further at this hypothesis. If we rotate any object having mass, or weight if you prefer, we will develop a certain amount of force. Every bit of mass that lies outside the exact centerline of the rotating object will develop some amount of force unto itself. The amount of the mass and the peripheral speed of its movement will determine the amount of that force, according to the laws of centrifugal force. Also, according to those same laws, the effort exerted by the rotating mass will focus on a point directly away from the center of rotation. We have only to equalize the masses on all sides of the centerline around which they rotate. A like force on the other side must directly equal any force on one side of the centerline. So long as the forces generated on all sides of the centerline are equal, we have balance.

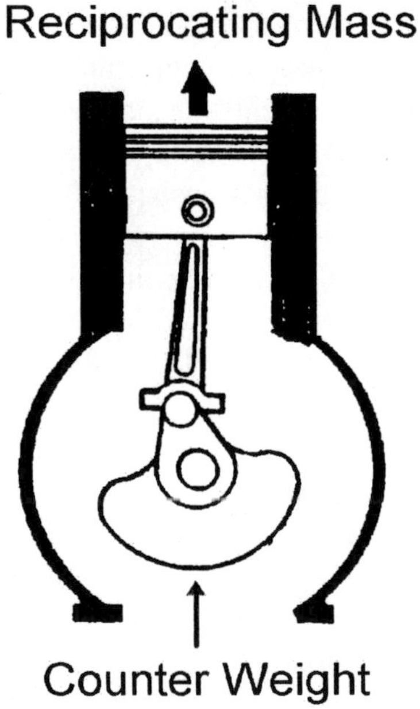

Figure 7

The counter weight on the crankshaft reduces the felt

vibration.

This is true of any rotating object. How do these rules apply specifically to the crankshaft of an engine? Let us assume a two-cylinder diesel engine for simplicity and proceed with this as a model. This is a 180-degree crankshaft and it is an inherently balanced design.

The crankshaft has a centerline or axis around which it rotates. We are looking directly along this axis from the timing gear end. Here we can see two arms that support the connecting rod journals. These arms have approximately equal size and approximately equal weight.

They are positioned exactly 180 degrees away from each other and should apply equal forces to the opposite sides of the crankshaft. This is a good spacing of the masses and consequently of the forces to be developed.

Now look on those sides opposite the crankshaft arms. Here we see a pair of semicircular weights cast into the crankshaft.

These weights also lie on opposite sides of the crankshaft from each other. If their weights are equal, they should also balance without further consideration. The counterweights are quite heavy and while they do balance each other, they also serve another purpose. We will get to that shortly. For the time being simply realize that every feature on one side of the crankshaft has a matching or opposing feature on the other side. The design anticipates a balanced condition and minor differences in the weight of opposing features can be equalized with a small removal or addition of weight during the balancing process.

So much for rotating parts and for their balance. Now let us look at reciprocating parts and consider the matter of counter balance. Reciprocating parts generate a linear force. These forces are moving in a straight line, towards and away from the crankshaft. These forces cannot be balanced.

Those reciprocating parts can only be counter balanced. To counter balance a force that moves in any given direction, we generate another opposing force to counter it. The counter force does not cancel out the original force; in fact, it exactly doubles the total load. If these opposing forces are attached at any single point, the sum of the two forces will be applied to that point, when the linear motion is brought to a stop.

How do these principles apply to a crankshaft? The counter weights on the crankshaft will develop the counter force that equalizes the effects of a moving piston. They do this by the manner of their location on the crankshaft and the nature of their movement in relationship to the piston. The piston goes up and the counter weight comes down. The piston goes down and the counter weight comes up. They will reach top dead center or bottom dead center at exactly 180 degrees away from each other. Thus the counter weight exactly counters the force of the moving piston. The problem lies in the fact that the load on the crankshaft itself is doubled by this effort. Both force and counter force are applied to the crankshaft.

The size of the counterweight on the crankshaft gives us a clue as to just how much force is required to counter the linear forces of the moving pistons. The diesel piston is quite heavy and it requires a substantial counter weight to counter balance the forces it generates.

This is another problem for the diesel engine. In fact it is a problem for any reciprocating piston engine. The piston starts and stops twice on each revolution of the engine. At the top of the stroke and at the bottom of the stroke the piston stops, then starts again.

A great deal of energy is required to make these starts and stops and every bit of that energy is a loss. To counter weigh the forces generated by these starts and stops just doubles that loss. How significant is the loss involved? I can tell you the figures which I have for a popular 392 cubic inch automobile engine shows a force of 5 tons is required to stop the piston at either end of the stroke and start it again. That is a great deal of wasted energy.

Yet the alternative is unacceptable in terms of vibration. Even though the forces generated by parts which move in a straight line are not actually diminished by the process of counter balance, PERCEIVED VIBRATION or FELT VIBRATION, that which our senses react to is greatly reduced.

The process of countering those linear forces vastly improves the comfort of the operator or passengers in any vessel.

To round out this Chapter, let us actually go through the process of balancing our two-cylinder engine. First, all of the parts must have equal weight. The pistons with rings, wrist pins, and pin locks must weigh the same. The connecting rods must also weigh the same but they must balance at both ends.

Since a portion of the connecting rod goes around with the crankshaft, the big ends of the rods must balance. A portion of the connecting rod moves up and down with the piston also, thus the little ends of the rods must balance as well.

The crankshaft must be rotated on a balance machine and it must balance internally and of itself. A weight equal to the big end of the connecting rod and the insert bearing must be added to the rod journals and the whole assembly rotated and rechecked for balance. If both of these checks are satisfactory, we have rotating balance.

There remains only to counter balance the engine. Weights, which represent the force to be generated by the piston and remainder of the reciprocating assembly, are attached to the crankshaft and the shaft is spun again. If the counter balance is correct the shaft is balanced.

Understand this: There are many degrees of balance employed with the various engines in use today. Some engines may have only a weight balance in which the total weight of the rods, the pistons, and other parts are matched but only limited effort is made to address the matter of counter balance. Furthermore, the exact procedure for balancing the engine varies from company to company and from one after-market practitioner to another. The factories balance a new engine to allowable limits and the stray forces, which are caused by small amounts of imbalance, are controlled in their intensity to satisfy those limits.

The flywheel and the drive plate are bolted to the crankshaft and rotate with it. Yet they are seldom included directly in any balancing process. Rather their state of balance is established to a standard that is considered close enough for mass production.

There are few instances when a factory actually balances a flywheel with the crankshaft. They are much more likely to do so if the flywheel is to be sold with the engine.

The harmonic balancer also is attached to and rotates with the crankshaft. This is a vital piece of every engine and it may in fact have an improper name. The harmonic balancer does not balance anything. Rather it generates forces that break up certain destructive vibration patterns in the engine. By so doing, it literally saves the engine from itself. Harmonic balancers must always be in place on the engine, they must be kept in good order, and the engine must never be operated with a faulty harmonic balancer.

If your propeller shaft is straight and perfectly aligned, your propeller is also balanced, but your driveline still has an elusive vibration, check the harmonic balancer. It may not be the problem but it is certainly capable of doing so.

Despite the difference in the general approach to balance which diverse companies or individuals may employ, the overall procedure is much as I have described it. If you have a good grasp of the principles involved that will be sufficient for me to declare this Chapter a success.

Later in this book I discuss vibration as an entity. Vibration is a large consideration for any engine but the diesel generates a great deal of this potentially destructive force. We will explore the sources as well as the remedies for this interesting phenomenon.

Balance is truly achieved through opposition and opposing forces. Go to the nearest shop and ask to see a crankshaft. Look at the arm, the counter weight, and the other features, including the journals and bearing surfaces. Get a good feeling for how the crankshaft performs its job and you will have a new respect for this hard working part of your engine.

CHAPTER EIGHT
COMPRESSION & IGNITION

Compression, as it relates to the operation of the diesel engine, is the act of squeezing air into a smaller space than it originally occupied. The movement of the piston from bottom dead center to top dead center, with the valves closed, effects this squeezing. The comparative volumes of the cylinders control the amount of pressure achieved within the cylinders of the diesel.

We refer to these comparative volumes in terms of their ratio to each other. The mathematical comparison, once made, is generally referred to as the compression ratio. The volume at bottom dead center is always greater than remains at top dead center and the numerical expression of that ratio is influenced accordingly.

How is the compression ratio for a diesel engine established? Begin with the piston at bottom dead center and measure the total volume of the cylinder, including the combustion chamber. Raise the piston to top dead center and measure the volume of the combustion chamber alone. The ratio between these two volumes is the compression ratio.

As an example. Suppose that we have 96 cubic inches of volume in the overall measurement at bottom dead center. Further the combustion chamber alone has 5 cubic inches of volume inside its confines. The ratio between 96 cubic inches and 5 cubic inches is the compression ratio for that cylinder.

It would be a bit awkward to give the compression

ratio as 96:5 so we reduce the numbers to the lowest decimal. Use this calculation to solve the proportion: 96/5 = X/1. Solving this simple equation by cross-multiplying, 5 X = 96 and then dividing, we see that X = 19.2. Thus our compression ratio is 19.2: 1.

What does that tell us about the cylinder pressure?

The air pressure at sea level is generally conceded to be 14.7 pounds at standard barometer. If we began with an open cylinder, the air pressure within that cylinder would be 14.7 pounds and we refer to this as one atmosphere of pressure. Now close the valves and raise the piston. What is the result?

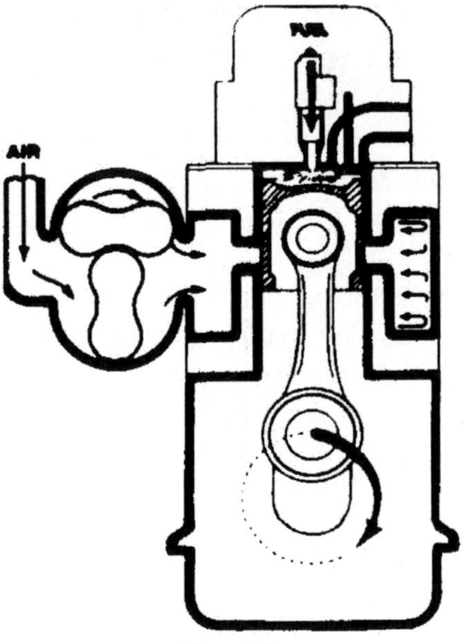

Figure 8
Courtesy of Detroit Diesel

The diesel engine at the moment of ignition.

With the compression ratio given in multiples of a known (atmospheric) pressure, assume we have only to multiply. Atmospheric pressure is 14.7 pounds, multiply this figure by 19.2 times (atmospheres) and we see that 14.7 X

19.2 = 282.24 pounds per square inch. This is a theoretical figure and the actual result of rotating the engine will be a higher pressure, considerably higher. Why is this so? The answer lies in a known physical reaction.

Remember the heat factor we discussed earlier in the book? The higher is the pressure exerted upon a gas, the hotter it will become and the faster we exert that pressure the even greater will be the temperature rise. As the piston rises and pressure is exerted upon the air in the cylinder, the temperature in the cylinder will rise accordingly. This temperature rise will cause the air to expand. This expansion will add to the growing pressure within the cylinder as the two processes, compression and expansion feed upon each other. It is possible to calculate, with a considerable degree of accuracy, exactly how much temperature rise will result from 19.2 atmospheres of compression, or any other amount for that matter, at any given number of rpm's.

It is not the intent of this dissertation to become involved with complicated formulae. Therefore, I will not pursue this further. What I do want you to understand is generally how compression ratios are calculated, what is the effect of compression on the air in the cylinder, and how this relates to the firing of the diesel.

Do not forget the time factor. Compression creates heat and the faster the act of compression occurs; the greater will be the increase in temperature. Said another way, "The faster the engine rotates, the hotter the air in the cylinder. The hotter the air becomes, the better the fuel will burn."

This alone, if no other reason, makes it necessary for the diesel to have a very good starter motor, and to rotate at a good speed on the starter. It also speaks to the need for good batteries in the electric start engine. Lazy batteries may not turn the engine very rapidly and while this is bad in warm weather, it can lead to total silence in cold weather. When very cold air enters the cylinder of the diesel it will need more degrees of temperature change to ignite the new charge of fuel. Thus it will require the fastest possible cranking speed to reach ignition temperature.

You must understand those high compression ratios employed for the firing of the diesel are not, of themselves, the source of great power but they are the source of the heat that makes the engine run. There are several things I want to touch on.

First, the compression ratios of diesel engines tend to vary widely. Light duty engines tend to have comparatively low compression ratios, some as low as 15: 1. These engines may need help in starting since the engine may not create enough heat from compression alone to accomplish initial ignition.

Over the years there have been many devices employed to accomplish this purpose. One of these which is still in common use today is the glow plug. The glow plug is nothing more than a small heater. It employs a wire coil in a metal body, screwed into the cylinder of the engine.

The system is not unlike the small electric heater you may have in your bathroom. Current for this glow plug is furnished by the storage battery that cranks the engine. When the engine has started, the glow plug is turned off, and residual heat in the cylinder is now sufficient to maintain operation.

There have been some truly unique ideas for starting diesel engines. One of these was the match start diesel. This engine employed a "T" shaped handle on a device that screwed into the cylinder head. At the end of the device was a small cup and into this cup went a match which was made of a material resembling the punk we use to light our firecrackers. You insert a plug of this punk into the cup, set a match to the plug, and screw it into the cylinder head. This punk like material gave of a set of low temperature sparks which aided initial combustion.

There was also a hothead diesel. This engine had a series of cups indented into the cylinder head. The engineer or deck hand used a blowtorch to heat these cups to substantial temperatures before the engine could be started. With a hot spot in the cylinder head, ignition came easily.

Both match start and hothead diesels took inordinate amounts of time to start and both systems have been largely abandoned. Yet they were in vogue at one time and I will never forget the first match start engine I encountered. Had it not been for an old timer who had worked on that old tug for years and years, I would never have figured out how to get power on the engine.

The last low compression odd ball I will tell you about is the dual compression diesel engine that has both spark plugs and a carburetor. This engine starts on gasoline with a compression relief system. This system employs a lever-operated shaft with fingers attached. The shaft is rotated manually and those fingers depress the compression release valves, holding them off their seats and dropping cylinder pressures to gasoline engine levels. The engine starts and runs on gasoline for a few seconds. Then as the cylinders warm up to temperature it is converted over to diesel fuel.

You have now heard a great deal about low compression diesel engines what about the other variety? They too have their eccentricities. The high compression engine will run off anything that will burn. Would you believe, bunker oil? Bunker oil is so thick that it has to be heated to temperatures as high as 300 degrees to enable the pumps to carry it. This material may be as high as 0.05 percent sulfur ash yet it will fire readily under the heat of high compression. Diesel engines have been manufactured with compression ratios as high as 30: 1 and at the temperatures these engines produce they will even burn coal.

That probably sounds like a flight into fancy for most readers but the Chinese actually built a diesel that burned a slurry of coal dust and water. It was actually a practical engine and it served a needed purpose at a time when fuel oil was a scarce commodity in China.

Sure, these are extremes, far out, call them what you will but they are a part of the amazing history of the diesel engine. Between the extremes are a lot of every day engines that get little press but perform heroically, none the less.

The truly endearing thing about compression ignition is this: There are no parts to the ignition system. There are no points or condensers, there is no power pack, no coils, and in fact, no parts of any nature to break. Compression ignition occurs as a result of natural physical phenomena that stem from the rotation of the engine, the movement of the piston, and the resulting heat of the air/fuel mix.

In the early part of this chapter I made the remark that "The high compression ratios employed for the firing of the diesel are not the source of great power." I will expand upon this statement later.

After reading this chapter, besides a bit of history, I hope you have gained some feeling for compression, heat, and the operation of the diesel. I also hope you will begin to see why this is sometimes referred to as a heat engine as well as a compression ignition engine.

CHAPTER NINE
DIESEL INJECTORS

Diesel engines themselves are simplicity personified. They are straightforward and easily understood but the fuel injector systems that feed their cylinders are another matter. I am going to try to explain a complicated subject in the simplest terms possible.

Parts of this chapter will be repetitive. I have done this in an effort to achieve detail and clarity. Please bear with me and we will do this together.

Features of the diesel injector seem to come in threes. There are many different styles of fuel injectors but they can generally be categorized in three groups. They are Separate Unit Injectors, Direct Injectors, and Electronic Injectors. They all have three things in common. Let us begin with the three common features of all diesel injection systems.

First, there must be some form of low pressure, fuel supply pump. The second requirement is a high-pressure fuel supply pump and the third requirement is some type of injector. These three features are common to all injector systems. How do they work?

The low pressure, fuel supply pump supplies fuel to the high-pressure pump. This low-pressure pump must be capable of drawing fuel from the tank. The high-pressure fuel pump is generally called an injector pump. It receives the fuel from the low-pressure pump and raises that pressure many times.

It delivers the fuel to the injector nozzle at greatly

elevated pressures. The fuel is then driven through the injector nozzle and it is ultimately injected into the cylinder. These are the three common features of all injector systems. The differences between systems lie in how they accomplish this. Let us look at each individually.

THE SEPARATE UNIT INJECTOR

Begin with the Separate Unit Injector. This was the first type of injector ever built. It had an individual and separate low-pressure pump and a second individual high-pressure injection pump. Both units were mechanically driven.

A lobe drove the low-pressure pump on the camshaft and the high-pressure pump by an accessory drive attached to the timing gear. Both pumps were located alongside the engine.

In this system the low pressure fuel pump delivered fuel to the high-pressure injector pump. The high-pressure injector pump then raised the pressure to elevated levels and delivered the fuel, through long fuel lines, to the injectors. The injectors were also individual units and they were mounted atop the cylinders of the engine. These injectors delivered fuel to the cylinders. Thus there were three separate parts needed to accomplish this type of injection.

This was a very rugged system and gave excellent service. These injector systems are still quite popular today. They are common to the smaller as well as the larger diesels and there are literally millions of them still in use.

THE DIRECT INJECTOR

The second type of injector system is referred to as a Direct Injector. The direct injector employs the same three operations as the separate unit injector but it uses only two components to accomplish this. There is an individual, low pressure, fuel supply pump, just as before, but there is a Direct

Injection unit mounted atop the cylinders.

The direct injection unit contains the high pressure, injector pump and the injector nozzles in a single unit. The low-pressure fuel supply pump feeds diesel fuel to this Direct Injector. Inside the unit the high-pressure pump raises the pressure on the fuel to very high levels just as it did in the first system. However, there are no fuel delivery lines. The pressurized fuel passes directly through the injector and into the cylinder at the same time. This unit was popularized by General Motors or Detroit Diesels and has been growing in acceptance ever since.

A push rod and rocker arm operate the direct injector very much like a valve. The entire unit is mounted directly onto the cylinder head. This type of injector is not as old as the single unit system but it too is very efficient and quite well accepted. It is growing in popularity and it's numbers would have exceeded those of the Single Unit Injector, had it not been for the advent of the Electronic Fuel Injector.

THE ELECTRONIC FUEL INJECTOR

The third type of injector is the Electronic Diesel Injector. It too receives diesel fuel from a low-pressure supply pump. The electronic injector, like the direct injector, has the high-pressure pump and the injector nozzle in a single unit.

The electronic high-pressure fuel pump also raises the fuel pressure to a very high level and delivers it to the cylinder in a single operation. A major difference here is the use of an electromechanical, solenoid powered pump for injection.

Let us break down the function of each of these systems and examine their individual operations in greater detail.

We will begin with the first named and oldest style around, the separate pump/injector model. I will start with the operation of the low pressure, fuel supply pump.

This pump is normally a simple device with a

diaphragm and two, one way valves. It is driven off the camshaft of the engine in much the same manner as those pumps you are familiar with on the gasoline engine. The pressure generated by this low-pressure pump is seldom more than 5 lbs./in.^{2}.

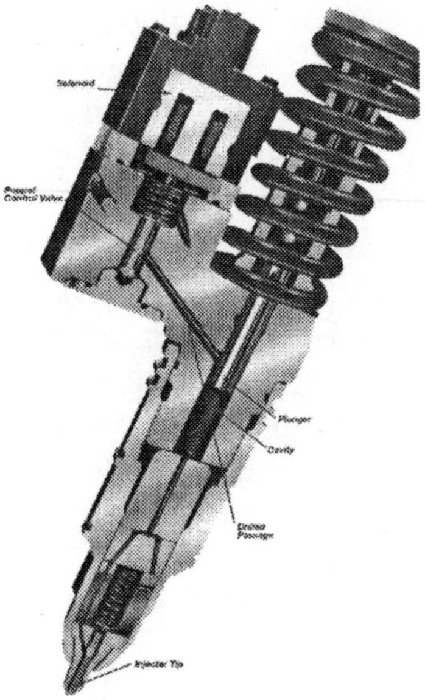

Courtesy Detroit Diesel
Figure 9

This illustration shows the parts of a diesel injector.

The separate, high pressure, injector pump is engine driven with a timed gear. It resides outside the engine and is mounted as an accessory. The pump body may be made of cast iron or aluminum but more commonly it is cast iron.

Inside the pump body is a camshaft with one or more lobes for each cylinder on the engine. There is generally one injector for each cylinder but larger engines may have two or even more. A series of bored holes in the pump body accommodate the plungers which actually pump the diesel fuel.

The bottom ends of these small plungers ride on the

camshaft lobes. As the camshaft lobe rotates it also raises the plunger and the plunger expels any fuel in the bored hole. That fuel is then delivered under great pressure to the injector (fuel) lines.

The fuel lines that deliver the fuel are made of very hard steel tubing and are all of an equal length. This equal length is maintained between the individual lines without regard to the distance from the injector pump to any individual injector. Only by maintaining this equal length can the injector deliver equal amounts of fuel to all of the cylinders in the engine.

The injector lines are made of very hard steel for several reasons. First they must handle extremely high pressures. Second, they are subjected to tremendous vibration caused by that fuel pressure which is alternately applied and removed. A third source of vibration occurs simply because they are attached to the engine which in itself creates substantial vibration. Those fuel delivery lines tend to develop sympathetic vibrations that are transmitted from the engine.

The highly pressurized fuel follows the injector lines and eventually enters the injector itself. The injector consists of a metal body made of cast iron. At one end is an orifice that receives the incoming fuel. At the other end is a nozzle that delivers fuel to the cylinder. This is the separate system.

Now let us look at the Direct Injector. The direct injector pump is a newer device although it has been around for more than 50 years. In this system a gear generally drives the low-pressure pump from inside the engine.

This pump is a trochoid pump and the internal parts are all metal. The pressures from this low-pressure pump are actually higher than those developed by the low-pressure pump on the separate system. This trochoidal pump delivers diesel fuel to a kind of fuel rail at about 90 lbs./in.^{2}.

The rail consists of a series of passages in the cylinder head, which carry the fuel to each individual injector. The injector has the high-pressure pump within the unit. It is driven by a mechanism that operates much the same as an overhead valve.

Visualize if you will the familiar automotive system. A camshaft located in the cylinder block operates a lifter. The lifter, in turn, operates a push rod that drives a rocker arm. On the other end of that rocker arm is the valve. Now substitute the injector for that valve. Viola, you have it.

The injector pump receives its fuel from the fuel rail and takes it into the pumping area. Here is a plunger much like that of the first system. The rocker arm drives the plunger down and fuel is driven out through the nozzle, into the cylinder. This is the direct injector system.

How about the Electronic Fuel Injector? The electronic fuel injector for the diesel engine closely resembles the FICHT injector, which is employed on the OMC outboard engines. The electronic diesel injector produces a great deal more pressure than does the FICHT unit but the general method of generating that pressure is much the same.

The low-pressure pump that feeds the Electronic Injection system delivers fuel to the high-pressure pump at about 100 lbs./in.^{2}. The High Pressure Pump is a unit or direct style that also has the high-pressure pump and the nozzle in a single entity. There are two major differences between this unit and other direct injector unit.

First, the electronic injector employs an electromechanical pump powered by a solenoid to create high pressure for injection. This system is interesting and its electrical nature leads to the second big difference between this and the purely mechanical injector.

A computer and the timing of the injector can control the electronic injector; the amount of fuel delivered and the rate of delivery can all be programmed into an Electronic Control Module or ECM.

This system has several advantages and we will enumerate those later. For now, let us go to the end of the injection chain and talk about the actual process of injection. At the point of injection, the process is much the same for all systems.

Every injector must have a nozzle or pintle through which fuel is delivered to the cylinder. Fuel from the injector pump must be held away from the cylinder until the exact propitious moment for injection and this is accomplished with a ball check valve, located behind the pintle.

The spring that holds this ball check valve in place has a measured tension. When the injector pressure is sufficient to overcome the spring tension, the fuel will be driven through the pintle or nozzle into the cylinder.

The pintle has a series of tiny holes drilled into its end through which fuel exits the pintle itself. These holes are small enough to atomize or break up the fuel as it passes into the cylinder. The shape and pattern of these holes decides how the plume or atomized fuel charge will be shaped when it enters the cylinder. The matter of fuel plumes is hotly debated among injector designers and with reason. The shape of the plume has considerable effect on the flame propagation characteristics of any engine and this is very important.

All right, let us run a typical diesel fuel injector through one complete cycle. Begin with the piston that is coming up on the compression stroke. There is a fresh charge of air only in the cylinder. Remember, because of high compression figures and the pressure that is present in the cylinder we have ignition temperature before the engine is ready to fire.

The low-pressure fuel pump has all ready delivered fuel to the high-pressure injection pump and all lines are full with no air present. Just before the piston reaches top dead center (about 20 degrees) the camshaft operates the injector pump and fuel pressure is raised to about 2,200 lbs./in.^{2}. When the fuel pressure exceeds the tension on the ball check valve the fuel will be discharged through the nozzle. There must be no air in the system, anywhere. If air is present in the system the air will cushion (give against) the pressure and the injector will not cycle. This condition is called air lock and it is one of the few things that will stop the diesel engine. The condition is corrected by bleeding the system. Again this is accomplished in much the same manner as bleeding a set of hydraulic brakes.

Thus far I have ignored the matter of governors on the diesel. Every engine has one and they are of two types. The Electronic Fuel Injector uses a set of limits imposed by the Electronic Control Module and specified by the programming of that module. The fuel delivery curve is eminently controllable from slowest idle to top speed. Any predetermined RPM level can easily be maintained, up to the load limit of the engine. Engines with outstanding fuel efficiency have emerged as a result of electronic controls. Pollution from the diesel engine has been severely reduced.

All other diesel injectors employ some type of weight-and-spring arrangement. The weights are anchored on a pin at one end and restrained by a spring at the other. As the system rotates centrifugal force drives the weights out at the free end, causing them to stretch the spring restraint. When the engine slows down, the spring tension returns the weight to its original position against the reduced amount of centrifugal force. This weight-and-spring system uses a set of levers to control engine speed. It is very effective and really quite simple.

Each of these fuel injection systems has their strong points and their problems. The two mechanical systems served well and honorably for many years and there are so many thousands of them out there that each will undoubtedly be seen for many years to come. Yet the electronic injector is the undisputed champ in versatility and function. This will surely be the wave of the future.

CHAPTER TEN
ACCESSORIES

Accessories for the diesel engine are similar in many aspects to those of the gasoline engine but there are a few significant differences. I will explain those differences and the reasons for them. Some of those differences are quite interesting.

Let us begin with starters for the diesel engine. Starters for the diesel are often powered by electricity from a storage battery, just like the starters for a gasoline powered engine but generally much heavier in construction. They employ a starter motor with an electromagnetic solenoid that serves two purposes.

When the starter switch is applied the solenoid pulls a lever and engages the starter gear into the teeth in the starter ring. The starter ring is located around the circumference of the flywheel. The same solenoid also energizes the starter motor.

The sudden engagement of the starter motor and the flywheel gear is a rather violent occurrence. There is a Bendix system to protect the parts from damage. The Bendix system employs a very heavy spring that is wound around the shaft and the starter gear uses the shock absorptive qualities of this spring to prevent damage at engagement.

As the starter motor begins to turn the starter gear, the flywheel also rotates and of course, the engine follows. The starter gear releases from the flywheel as soon as power to the starter is withdrawn. So far this sounds pretty ordinary but here the similarity ends. The diesel starter must develop much greater torque than is required for the gasoline engine and it must turn faster.

Diesel engines must have those high compression figures we have described in order to start or run. Thus a great deal more raw power is needed from the starter simply to turn the engine. Then the diesel needs to turn more rapidly than its gasoline powered brethren.

Figure 10
Courtesy of Detroit Diesel

The starter motor for a diesel engine requires great power to turn the engine. This places a substantial strain on the batteries. The motor is also far larger than a gasoline engine starter.

The heat needed to effect combustion in the diesel depends upon the speed of rotation of the engine. The faster it turns, the hotter the cylinder becomes. In fact a number of the newer Electronic Fuel Injectors (EFI) are programmed to deliver fuel to the engine only after a pre-described number of turns on the starter. This gives the engine an opportunity to generate good ignition temperatures before fuel is fed to the cylinders.

Remember those big puffs of smoke that you were accustomed to seeing in the exhaust of a diesel when it first cranked? Those were caused by fuel being fed from the injectors into the cylinders before the cylinder temperature was sufficient to ignite the fuel.

As soon as the engine warmed up the cylinder temperatures rose sufficiently to burn the fuel cleanly and the smoke disappeared. Of course, by that time the damage to the environment was already done. The dirty diesel is becoming a thing of the past.

Because the diesel starter must turn rapidly and handle heavy loads it often has higher voltage than an ordinary gasoline engine starter. Diesel starters, which require 24 volts or even 36 volts for their proper operation, have become quite common on diesel engines and the electric starters for engines above 500 horsepower are quite large.

Of course these starters are totally enclosed which means that they are sealed against fumes from the bilge and they are explosion proof which suggests that they will not produce a spark during operation. FUMES FROM DIESEL FUEL ARE DANGEROUS!! Do not be lulled into the common belief that, "Diesel fuel is safe. It ain't like gasoline. You ain't gotta worry about it blowin' up on ya." Yes, diesel fuel is less volatile but under the proper conditions it will go up in spectacular fashion. Please believe me, I have been right on the spot when it did so, more than once.

An alternative to electric starters for the diesel is the air-powered starter. This is an excellent system that lasts a long time and operates, for the most part, without problems. The air starter is designed much like the devices that power an air drill or grinder. They consist of a motor that is operated by air pressure. They employ a Bendix system similar to the electrically powered starter but they have no potential to start a fire or set off any fumes present in the bilge. They have several disadvantages however.

First, they are expensive to purchase. Second, they are more expensive to repair. And third they require a substantial amount of air to operate them. That air must come from a reservoir. This reservoir must accept high pressures and hold a substantial amount of air.

Because of the amount of air needed to turn the diesel engine for even a few revolutions, this voracious need for air can be a problem if the engine is hard to start or develops an air lock. This air must come from a compressor and, of course, the compressor must have some source of power itself.

A small separate engine may be required for larger diesels while an accessory compressor mounted on the generator may be sufficient in many cases. Wherever the compressor gets its power, the power source must be independent of the main engine so the air supply can be replenished independently of the main engine.

Caterpillar and certain other diesels once employed a donkey motor to start the engine. The donkey motor was a small, gasoline-powered engine with a manual Bendix the operator engaged by hand. The smaller engine started the main diesel and was then shut down.

This system was generally used for earth movers and similar applications but it is worthy of mention simply for your information. A supply of gasoline was needed to fuel the donkey engine and that supply of gasoline could be a hazard in the confines of a closed engine room on a vessel.

There have been some diesel engines that were started by feeding compressed air directly to selected cylinders in the engine. This system required a great deal of air under very high pressure and some means of storing that air supply. This system is seldom seen today.

Alternators or generators for the diesel recognize the greater need for starting current and other increased power drains. They are generally higher capacities than those on the gasoline engine. These alternators or generators are also totally enclosed and explosion proof units.

Cooling systems for the diesel may employ raw water-cooling or closed circuit cooling. Raw water-cooling systems are straightforward. They simply employ a raw water pump, which pump seawater through the engine and manifolds to cool the entire unit.

Closed circuit cooling systems are a bit more complicated. They are of two separate styles. These are the heat exchanger system and the keel cooled system. The heat exchanger is the most common and we will address it first.

The heat exchanger itself is the heart of this system and it does exactly what the name implies. It exchanges the greater heat from the operating engine for the lesser heat of the raw seawater. How does it do this? Visualize if you will an automotive radiator. The radiator is connected to the engine with two hoses. A circulating water pump delivers the heated coolant to the radiator where it passes through a series of thin tubes. Air circulated through those tubes reduces the temperature of the coolant and returns it to the engine.

The radiator is, in fact, a heat exchanger that employs a coolant in a closed circuit. It reduces the temperature of the coolant by transferring heat to the cooler air. The marine heat exchanger is no more than a radiator that uses seawater to reduce the temperature of the engine coolant instead of air.

Again, visualize the automotive radiator with its thin coils. Wrap a metal covering or jacket around that radiator. Install a pair of tubes into that jacket to permit the entrance and exit of seawater. The raw water pump delivers a volume of sea water to the jacket and out of the discharge tube. Now we have raw seawater substituted for air but doing the same job. The automobile radiator or heat exchanger is air cooled while the marine heat exchanger is water-cooled.

In a radiator, heat is dissipated to the atmosphere. In a heat exchanger it is dissipated to the seawater. There are many similarities between heat exchanger cooling and keel cooling but there are enough differences to be worth mentioning.

Keel cooling also employs a heat exchanger but it has no outer jacket. The keel cooler is anchored to the hull along the line of, and to one or both sides of, the keel of the vessel. It consists of a series of tubes which contain the engine coolant and has the outside of those tubes exposed to the seawater.

This system very closely resembles the operation of the automotive radiator in many ways. It has no jacket and thence no raw water pump. Water circulates directly between the tubes of this system just as air circulates between the tubes of a radiator.

There are many advantages to the keel cooler. It does not require a separate pump to cool and this is one less part to break down. It is generally very reliable if the capacity of the system is sufficient for the engine to.

There are a few problems with this system also. First, the drag of the cooling unit is substantial as the vessel is driven through the water and this generally restricts the use of a keel cooler to slow moving, displacement vessels.

Second but still significant is the matter of the idling engine. When the vessel is stationary there is little flow of seawater around the tubes of the heat exchanger and the engine could overheat. This is a very real danger and because of the tendency to leave a diesel on standby or for other reasons, the keel cooler must have sufficient capacity to handle the idling engine.

The small diesel engine such as those employed as sailboat auxiliaries, are often raw water-cooled. They use only the direct water of the sea and circulate it throughout the entire system but few engines above 25 horsepower use this raw water-cooling. There is the matter of construction. Engines with wet sleeves or dissimilar metals used in the construction do not need exposure to an electrolyte (saltwater). They simply will not function for any length of time with raw water-cooling and so the method of construction restricts many diesels to closed circuit cooling.

The diesel engine employs a heat exchanger on the crankcase oil as well as the coolant. This system works in a similar manner to the system employed with the engine coolant except the crankcase oil is passing through the heat exchanger instead of coolant.

This system serves two purposes. It helps to keep lubricant temperatures at an acceptable level and it also helps to cool parts of the engine the coolant does not normally reach. Gasoline engines may or may not employ a heat exchanger on the crankcase lubricant but the diesel is seldom seen without one.

The tachometer on the diesel engine is handled differently from that of a gasoline engine since there is no coil and no spark to drive the tach. Cable driven tachometers with a drive similar to an automobile speedometer are common on the diesel. Tachometers driven by an electronic sending unit incorporated in the alternator are also common.

The same type of electronic sending unit may be directly driven by an accessory drive on the engine. These tachometers are worthy of your consideration. If you are interested in the concept, visit your nearest repower center.

CHAPTER ELEVEN
HOW A DIESEL OPERATES

Diesel engines generally fall into two categories, the two-stroke diesel and the four-stroke diesel. There are numerous similarities between the operation of the two engines but there are also substantial differences. The two-stroke diesel differs again in operation from the two-stroke gasoline engine.

I want to demonstrate those similarities as well as the differences. Because of the intriguing features of the two-stroke diesel, I am going to begin there. First I will briefly review the operation of a two-stroke, gasoline engine, move along to the comparison with the two-stroke diesel engine, and then I will offer a comparison between two-stroke and four-stroke diesels.

TWO-STROKE GASOLINE VERSUS TWO STROKE DIESEL

The two-stroke gasoline engine is principally represented in the marine field by the common outboard engines we are so familiar with. As you probably know, the two-stroke outboard first takes air or air/fuel mix into the crankcase. Whether air or air/fuel mix is present, there must also be oil for lubrication. The falling piston creates pressure in the crankcase. Then the entire mass, air/fuel/oil, is transferred to the combustion chamber, when the intake port opens.

Crankcase compression causes the engine to breathe. It is the reason we are able to charge the cylinders on the two-stroke outboard.

A two-stroke diesel has no such crankcase compression. There is no natural way to get air into the cylinders. There were many that said it would not breathe and it could not run. Millions of Detroit or General Motors diesels have proved them wrong. The secret to this engine lies in the scavenger blower that is mounted on the side of the engine.

This blower is gear driven and furnishes air to the cylinders. The Detroit Diesel is a good example of this type of engine and I will run you through a cycle in the life of this legendary power plant. As you will see, that blower is the sole reason for its performance.

Begin with the power stroke. Fuel has ignited in the cylinder, there is substantial pressure on the piston and it is being forced downward. The injector will continue to spray fuel into the cylinder for the remainder of the power stroke. This continuous spray is the basis for the constant pressure, diesel principle.

Part way down the power stroke the injector will cease to feed fuel to the cylinder and pressure will fall off. The exhaust valves will open and the burnt gasses will begin to exit the cylinder. The piston will continue down the stroke, though no further power is being developed inside.

The Detroit engine has no intake valves but rather it employs a series of intake ports. These ports are holes in the bores that are located at specially timed positions around the cylinders. There is an air chamber that surrounds the cylinder and air is provided to this chamber under pressure. The scavenger blower creates that pressure. When the piston clears the intake ports, air is forced into the cylinder. This activity takes the place of the transfer cycle on the outboard. The exhaust valves are still open and fresh air is entering the cylinder but there is no loss of unburned fuel. Remember on the diesel there is no fuel present, only air until the injector pops.

When the cylinder is clear the exhaust valve closes but the intake ports are still open. Pressure from the blower packs the cylinder and the piston starts to rise on the compression stroke. When the intake ports are covered by the piston we again have a closed cylinder and compression pressure begins to build in earnest.

At about 20 degrees before top dead center the heat and pressure in the cylinder will be at very high levels. The injector will pop and the cycle begins again. In this model we have intake and compression strokes on a single movement of the piston. We also have power and exhaust strokes on a single movement of the piston.

This is a 360-degree engine with a power impulse on every revolution or each 360-degree rotation of the crankshaft. It is not an RPM engine like the two-stroke outboard. The two-stroke diesel incorporates the long stroke, under square cylinder configuration of the true diesel and it has excellent torque capabilities.

Enterprise, Fairbanks Morse and other manufacturers have built two-stroke diesels that powered tugboats, submarines, and many other vessels with heavy-duty power requirements. Most of the oil field boats I ran in the oil fields were powered by the Detroit Diesel engine and these two-stroke engines gave excellent longevity.

While outboard engines and diesel engines alike share the ported cylinder and the two-stroke cycle, that is the end of the similarity. The two-stroke diesel engine is in fact a high compression, long stroke, gorilla while the outboard engine is a high speed, high performance, rhesus by comparison.

FOUR-STROKE GASOLINE VERSUS FOUR-STROKE DIESEL

The four-stroke diesel engine has most but not all of the attributes of its gasoline-powered counterpart. It operates on the common four-stroke principle with a separate intake, compression, power, and exhaust stroke, spread over two revolutions of the engine.

Since there is only one power stroke for every two revolutions of the engine, both four-stroke power plants are often referred to as 720-degree engines. This engine fires only once every second revolution. The two-stroke diesel fires every revolution or twice as often.

The two-stroke engine has twice as many power strokes, does it have twice the horsepower? "No." There is a reason for this and we will detail that reason in a later chapter on the mechanics of diesel engines.

Let us return to the matter of four-stroke diesel operation and run through one full cycle of the engine. Begin with the engine on the power stroke. Fuel is burning in the cylinder and pressure is driving the piston downwards. The injector is spraying fuel into the cylinder and pressure on the piston is continuous. Again, this is the constant pressure principal at work.

The piston is driven further downward, the injector ceases to feed fuel to the cylinder, the pressure begins to drop and the exhaust valve opens. Now the piston passes bottom dead center and starts up on the exhaust stroke. The burned gasses are discharged from the cylinder and the intake valve opens.

The exhaust valve closes and the piston starts down on the intake stroke. A fresh charge of air only is drawn into the cylinder. The intake valve closes and the piston starts up on the power stroke. The injector pops and the process begins again.

COMMON FEATURES OF ALL DIESEL ENGINES

There are several common features of all diesel engines. First, there is no throttle on the air intake. Second, there is no choke. Third, only air enters the engine through the intake valve or intake ports. Fourth, the power is controlled by the injector pump and directly relates to the amount of fuel the injector provides to the cylinder.

There is a problem common to all diesel engines that only the electronic injector is able to address. The mechanical injection systems, whether they be direct or separate pumps, may overload the engine with fuel under certain conditions. When the throttle is opened the mechanical injector provides more fuel to the engine. It does this whether the engine is capable of burning the entire amount or not. When the engine is heavily loaded and the throttle advanced rapidly, the injector can feed more fuel to the engine than the cylinder can burn. Heavy black smoke and a terrible odor accompany this situation. As engine RPM climb and the engine catches up the increased amount of fuel will be consumed, power will increase, and the smoke will disappear. If the engine is continuously overloaded this extra fuel, can be a real problem.

The excess fuel may wash the cylinders down, removing the lubricant and causing the pistons to gall or stick. The electronic fuel injector has numerous sensors that determine the load condition of the engine. It is better able to sense the needs of the engine and feed only the appropriate amount of fuel to the cylinders.

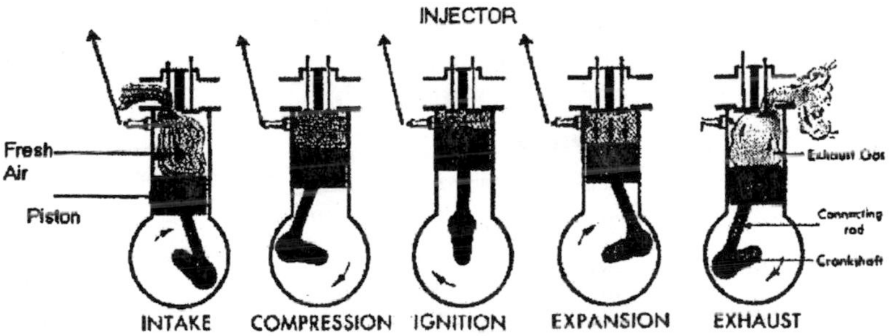

Figure 11

The five stages of a four-stoke diesel.

We have discussed the two-stroke and four-stroke diesel engines but this still begs a part of diesel lore. That part has to do with cylinder configuration. Diesel cylinders have been configured in all manner of strange shapes. The common in-line engine appears in the diesel parade, just as the "V" cylinder bank does. Yet Diesels have been manufactured as opposed piston engines as well.

In this configuration the cylinders appear in two banks, 180 degrees apart. This type of engine has been popularized in automobiles by such cars as the Corvair and the Volkswagen, both air-cooled engines.

The opposed piston or pancake engine is not seen in gasoline powered inboards but it is fairly common in diesel engines. Other diesels may have double acting cylinders in which a combustion chamber appears above and below the piston. There was a Fairbanks Morse engine that had two pistons in one combustion chamber. They faced away from each other and the engine even had two crankshafts.

These are not common shapes for the diesel engine but they have been used in the past.

Truth be told, there is almost no purpose to which the diesel engine has not been applied on one occasion or another. The German Hienkel Corporation even utilized diesel engines in some of their aircraft.

From the depths of the sea to the height of the clouds, diesel engines have powered our many conveyances. What a storied life they have lead. There is a certain romance that appends to the diesel and I wonder what Herr Diesel would say if he could see where his invention has gone.

If you have read this chapter on diesel engines carefully and if you are familiar with the operation of gasoline fueled engines you will immediately see that the manner of ignition and the manner of fuel/air intake are the major differences between the operational features of the two engines.

Go over this chapter more than once and try to visualize the sequence of events. The things that are moving and working in the engine at all times. When you have a good understanding of this information you will be able to see what is happening in the engine at any given time.

You will also have a good feeling for what is NOT going on if the engine fails. This understanding of what is missing is the cornerstone of all good trouble shooting. But that is another chapter.

CHAPTER TWELVE
MATHEMATICS & MECHANICS

The next subject I would like to introduce is turbo-charging the engine. First I want to do a bit of mathematics and discuss a few principles of mechanics. I will keep the math as simple as possible and most of the mechanics will be easily understood.

When we have this background to work with we will attack the subject of turbo-charging next. For now I want to approach those principles which apply to all engines and then see how they are effected by the addition of a turbocharger.

In this discussion we will be often concerned with the displacement of a diesel engine. Cubic inches of displacement are the common measurement used for describing displacement. It is further described as the swept volume of all the cylinders. Both terms are correct.

What does it mean? Visualize if you will a soda can. The top of the can is the top of the piston at top dead center in the cylinder bore. The bottom of the can is the top of the piston at bottom dead center in the cylinder bore. The sides of the can are the cylinder walls. The CONTENTS of the can are the number of cubic inches which will be DISPLACED as the piston moves from bottom dead center to top dead center, traveling up the bore. So much for DISPLACEMENT; how about SWEPT VOLUME?

The VOLUME of the can will be SWEPT clean by the passage of the piston as it moves from bottom dead center to top dead center. Thus the term swept volume. Swept volume is also equal to the contents of the can. For any practical purpose, cubic displacement and swept volume are equivalent terms and either term is an appropriate description.

Why are they important? Displacement is the only fair way to compare two engines, whether gasoline to gasoline, diesel to diesel, or gasoline to diesel, cubic inches is the standard most accepted by every racing organization in the world for comparing two engines.

That having been said, how do we calculate cubic inches of displacement? There is a simple sounding formula for this calculation. It appears as:

$$(A \times L) \times N = D$$

In this model we see that A is the area of the piston top in square inches. L is the length of the stroke.

Multiply A x L and you have the cubic inches for a single cylinder. Now N is the number of cylinders and when this has been multiplied by the results of the first calculation, we get the total number of cubic inches for the entire engine.

There is a small problem here. This formula requires the mathematician first calculate the area of the piston surface before he proceeds and that requires more effort. Let us try another model. I really prefer the following formula:

$$B \times B \times S \times .785 \times N = D$$

In this model B is the bore, S is the stroke, .785 is a constant, and N is the number of cylinders. Lets us see how this works with an engine of known dimensions. Try a Westerbeke 4-91 that has 4 cylinders with a bore listed as 2.8745 and a stroke of 3.5.

Using the above formula we have (B) 2.8745 x (B) 2.8745 x (S) 3.5 x .785 x (N) 4 = 90.8 cubic inches. This is an unusual situation since most factories round off numbers and usually introduce at least some error but the factory advertised displacement for this engine is exactly 90.8 cubic inches.

Try the Perkins 4-108 with a bore of 3.125 and a stroke of 3.5.

Okay we know how to calculate the number of cubic inches an engine will displace, why does it matter? To answer that question, let us examine the manner in which the engine works. We can create a mythical engine for ourselves and we will call this guy Powerful Pal. Pal has a bore diameter of 4.0 inches and a stroke with a length of 5.0 inches.

How much horsepower will Pal develop? We have a very simple formula which says that:

$$Tq \times RPMs / 5252 = HP$$

In this formula we see that Tq (Torque) multiplied by RPMs (Revolutions Per Minute) and divided by the constant 5252 = Horsepower. This is what the dynamometer does. It measures developed torque from the engine and keeps a count of the RPMs.

The multiplication is then an easy calculation. Let us assume a figure of 388 lbs/ft of developed torque and place the RPMs at 2,200. Multiplying these two together and divide by 5252. We see that Pal develops 162.528 horsepower.

What does this have to do with cubic inches? Begin with the power stroke and pressure on top of the piston. As before, we measure pressure in $lbs./in.^2$ For this demonstration let us assume 150 $lbs./in.^2$. If we have pounds per square inch in cylinder pressure given, we will need to know, "To how many square inches are we are applying this pressure?"

What is the area in square inches of the piston top? Try this formula:

$$\text{Area} = \text{Pi} \times \text{Radius squared}$$

or

$$A = \pi R^2$$

In this model the value for Pi (π) is a constant, 3.1416, the Radius of the circle is half the diameter and 1/2 of four is 2 so we now have 3.1416 x 2 x 2 = the area of the piston top. Our Pal has an area of 12.402 square inches.

Now if we multiply the pressure in lbs./in.^{2} times the number of square inches we find there are 150 x 12.402 square inches or 1,863 lbs./in.^{2}in total pressure on the piston top. Obviously this total pressure relates directly to the size of the bore which decides how many square inches of surface are present. More square inches, more total pressure, and vice versa.

How about the stroke? The stroke is the distance the piston travels in a complete cycle from top dead center to bottom dead center. For Pal this distance is 5.0 inches. Since the crankshaft turns over 180 degrees during any full stroke, the stroke is twice as long as the arm on the crankshaft.

The arm on the crankshaft is 2.5 inches and the length of that arm is a vital part of the engine design. The length and the pressure on the piston top decides how much torque the engine will develop. Before we try to calculate torque figures for Pal, let us explore the nature of torque itself.

Torque is a potential. Torque, of itself, does no work. If we a take a shaft and attach a 1 foot lever to this shaft, then apply a force of 1 pound to that lever, exactly 1 foot from the centerline of the shaft, we will get 1 foot pound of torque. We write this as: 1 lb./ft.

The length of this lever or arm can be more or less than a foot in length and the torque resulting from the application of a given force will change proportionately. Pal has a 2.5 inch arm and 2.5 inches are equal to .2083 feet (divide 2.5 inches by the 12 inches in a foot.)

If we take the 1863 pounds of force applied to the piston top and apply it to our .2083 foot lever we get a figure of 387.499 or about 388 lbs./ft. of torque. That fits the model for horsepower that appeared in the first example, but this example is not exactly accurate.

The assertions made and the calculations themselves are quite accurate but we have violated a single mechanical principle. Force generated by pressure applied to the piston top is not directly applied to the crankshaft arm. The connecting rod applies that force at an angle.

Force applied at an angle develops a resultant that is the actual result caused by the indirect application. It is calculated according to a resolution of forces diagram and that calculation is going to be just a bit outside the scope of this discussion.

These are the things I really want you to remember from this chapter:

Burning fuel applies pressure to the piston top, the bigger the top of the piston, the more pressure. The smaller the piston, the less pressure.

The application of pressure on the top of the piston creates downward force transmitted to the arm of the crankshaft. That force creates torque and when the crankshaft begins to turn against a load, that torque, plus the RPMs the engine turns, is measurable as horsepower.

These concepts seem so simple when stated in this manner. Many of you who will read this book have been involved with engines in the past and I will try not to over simplify, however, I am trying to reach a mixed audience. If you are familiar with the principles described here, perhaps this book will help you to verbalize those things you already know.

If I can accomplish that goal alone this book will have been worth your reading. It is so very important for the mariner to be able to communicate with the mechanic and for the mechanic to be able to reciprocate. For those of you who are new to the world of diesel, I hope I am able to bring you some understanding of diesels.

CHAPTER THIRTEEN
NATURALLY ASPIRATED ENGINES VERSUS THE BOOST

We are about to delve into the field of high performance diesel engines. In bygone years it was believed that one-horsepower-per-cubic-inch represented a barrier that could never be surmounted by any diesel. Today we have passed this figure and the horsepower race continues, full-blown.

What are the characteristics of these high performance, oil burners? High cost, short life, and increased fuel consumption. This should come as no surprise since every one of those characteristics applies to any engine of any type which is designed to scintillate.

Are all blown engines designed for speed? Certainly not. Many industrial engines employ turbo chargers or superchargers for added power. The truth is a small boost from a blower adds a small amount of horsepower to the engine at a small increase in cost and a small loss of longevity. A large amount of boost from a blower adds a larger amount of horsepower at a much larger increase in cost and a much greater loss of longevity. How the blower works, why it works, and the tradeoffs are next.

In the last chapter we learned about the effects of cylinder pressure on the piston tops. We learned that more cylinder pressure generates more torque and finally, more horsepower. This cylinder pressure is directly effected by natural conditions.

A naturally aspirated engine uses only the existing pressure of the air around us to provide air to the cylinders of the engine. There is only 14.7 pounds of natural atmospheric pressure. There is a limit to how much air will enter the cylinder of the engine in the short time available for it to do so.

Figure 13 a

Detroit Diesel blower unit.

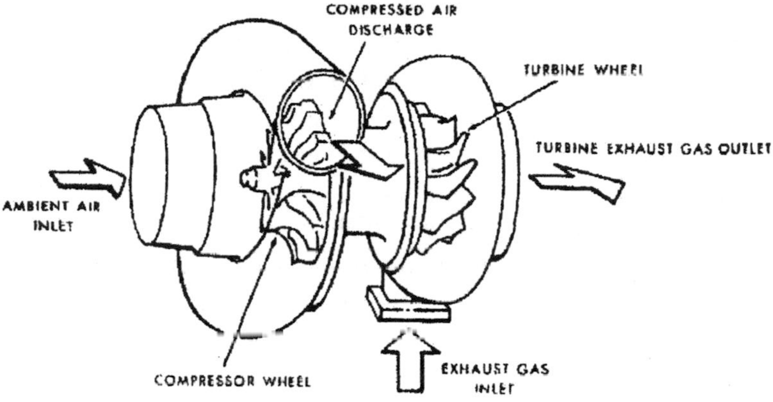

Figure 13b

Typical turbo unit.

A certain amount of air is required to burn any given quantity of fuel and as the amount of available air falls off, the amount of fuel the engine can effectively burn is reduced; less air, less fuel, less pressure in the cylinder. When this condition assaults the engine we say the engine has breathed out.

Look at the torque and horsepower curves for any given engine and you will see that, beginning at idle, the torque curve rises as the RPMs increase. Then at some point on the RPM scale the torque curve peaks or reaches it upper limit. This occurs when the engine breathes out or ceases to get the full charge of air the cylinders require.

Now there is not enough air. There is less pressure on the piston top, and the result is less torque. What to do? If we need more air in the engine and if we cannot get that air by natural means, why not force-feed the engine? Enter the booster, blower or turbo.

The blower or supercharger feeds additional air to the engine. It is either belt driven by a pulley on the crankshaft or gear driven from the crankshaft. The turbocharger also feeds additional air pressure to the engine but the turbocharger uses pressure from the exhaust to drive a turbine that provides the boost.

The diesel engine with a blower may produce exciting results. The blower can provide enough pressure to load the cylinders to the limit and beyond. The high performance diesel engines of the '90s are able to rival gasoline powered engines in terms of horsepower per cubic inch and even horsepower per pound.

Unfortunately, at high levels of boost they do not last a great deal longer than gasoline powered engines, but the reason for that will be explored more fully in a later chapter. Let us begin the serious part of this discussion with the operation of a blower.

Let us begin with the supercharger blower. This unit was most prevalent in the two-stroke diesel engines of the past. In the early carnation it was driven with a gear and often referred to as a scavenger blower. I discussed this system in the last chapter but there are a couple of things I did not touch upon.

The supercharger/scavenger is a concentric impeller, roots-type blower and it employs a pair of oblong, two lobed, rotors driven by perfectly timed gears to keep them synchronized. The rotors rotate in a twin lobed case that perfectly fits their outer periphery.

The rotor lobes have a flat sealing lip that is machined to very close tolerances. This lip very nearly drags the case, leaving a clearance of only 0.002 inch. This permits the rotors to displace air in a predetermined direction and to build considerable pressure in doing so. In fact the available pressure from the roots type blower can exceed 20 lbs./in.^{2}. This is quite enough pressure, when added to that of the atmosphere, to make gobs of horsepower. Yet the two-stroke, Detroit Diesel engines that we used for an example in our last chapter do not employ nearly so much pressure.

In fact, the pressures on these engines were quite modest and the engines were thought of as naturally aspirated engines for many years. Truth be told, the engines would not have run at all without the blower. The engines were long stroke, work horses and only produced about 1 horsepower per 2.36 cubic inches. This assumption is based upon 180 continuous horsepower from a 6-71, N series, Detroit Diesel w/426 cu. ins. displacement, for example. These are fairly representative numbers for the genre.

This was a modest figure. The average mechanic was inclined to accept these engines as naturally aspirated and the blower as a scavenger but for the sake of your knowledge, it did provide a small boost.

The roots type blower that General Motors adapted to their diesel engines was very efficient and received wide spread acceptance from sources outside the marine field. The automobile racing fraternity loved it; dragsters revered it.

Specially adapted units from B & M or other providers made the Gimmy Blower a household word. If you wanted more air from the blower, just speed up the RPMs a bit. It is quite evident that this blower had tremendous capabilities, though few of them have ever been used for high performance diesels.

The darling of the high performance diesel aficionado is the turbocharger. This system actually employs two turbines. The exhaust gasses exiting the engine drive the first turbine that powers the system. The second or driven turbine actually constitutes an air compressor that feeds air under pressure to the engines cylinders.

How much air will it feed? As much as you want, maybe more than you need, enough to improve the performance of the engine or literally destroy it in minutes. The turbo charger is the quickest way ever discovered by man to make cheap horsepower in large quantities.

How about back pressure? Every person who has ever worked on an engine knows that a restricted exhaust slows down and disturbs the breathing of the engine. Why does the turbo not do the same thing? The turbo actually does cost us something at low speeds. When the flow of exhaust gas is slow, the turbo charger does not create boost but rather drags against the engine, creating a back pressure on the cylinders and reducing the engine's efficiency. As the flow of exhaust gas increases the turbo charger spools up to 150,000 revolutions per minute, or beyond.

Now the compressor is feeding air pressure to the cylinders. When that pressure exceeds the normal pressure of the atmosphere the intake manifold will show boost. Boost should be recognized as a positive pressure, above that of the atmosphere. At this point the engine will show a very strong increase in power and performance.

Of course the amount of the boost decides how much increase in performance will occur. It also decides how much additional wear and tear is visited upon the hard working parts of the engine. Boosting the manifold pressure on the diesel can increase not only the cylinder pressure but the cylinder temperature as well.

Believe it or not there is a family of double boosted engines out there. Johnson and Tower, Stewart and Stevenson, and other similar companies produce the crown princes of the high performance field. These engines are built on the Detroit Diesel block and they employ a turbocharger that feeds a supercharger and uses both entities for boost.

If, as previously stated here, it is possible to get enough air from either the turbo charger or the supercharger to wipe the engine out, why then the dual system? Remember we also mentioned that the Detroit Diesel is a two-stroke and it would not run without the blower.

Since the turbo charger operates off exhaust gasses and there are no exhaust gasses available until the engine is running, the original blower is an absolute necessity. But believe this, "It also permits the creation of some very powerful engines of comparatively small displacement."

As an example? The Detroit, 6-71-N that we mentioned above and which developed 180 horsepower in its natural form will now produce 450 horsepower, under considerable boost. That is a 250 percent increase in performance.

We have changed from an engine that often pulled shrimp nets for 20,000 hours without overhaul to an engine that gets 30-knot speeds from a sport fisherman. The blower is a wizard, a Houdini that can change the entire performance of a diesel engine from mild to wild.

I will discuss the effects of turbo charging on the structure and components of the engine in a later chapter. For now, enjoy the idea that a staid and stolid diesel can become a fire-breathing monster. Just give it a boost.

CHAPTER FOURTEEN
FLAME PROPAGATION

This chapter is about flame propagation in the diesel engine. Let us begin with an understanding of the term itself. Flame propagation is the process of igniting the fuel within the cylinder and of adding fuel to those flames to build additional pressure. As fuel is added, the flames will propagate or involve additional droplets within the combustion chamber and across the surface of the piston. The trick to this effort is to add the additional fuel, build that added pressure and keep the entire process orderly and under control.

What constitutes control? The diesel engine runs on a controlled explosion. Confine a combustible material (diesel fuel) within a small space (the combustion chamber) under great heat and pressure (compression) and when you light it off the mixture is certain to explode. The entire matter of flame propagation is devoted to controlling the intensity of that explosion and the burn rate at which it occurs.

How do you control an explosion? The amount of pressure, heat and fuel added to the cylinder all add to or subtract from the effort.

This sets the stage for the next phase of our discussion. Some of you may already be aware of the manner in which flame propagation occurs in the gasoline engine however flame propagation is a totally different matter for a diesel engine. In general there are three major differences in the process. The manner in which air/fuel is introduced is the first difference.

The style of the combustion chamber is a second difference. The fuel distribution in and around that very different shaped chamber is a third difference. Let us approach these elements in the order of their introduction.

Remember that speed in the diesel engine is controlled by the amount of fuel that is provided to the engine. The diesel engine has no butterfly or air restrictor in the cylinder head or intake manifold. Consequently it gets a fairly full charge of air, even at idle speed. It also gets a very small amount of fuel.

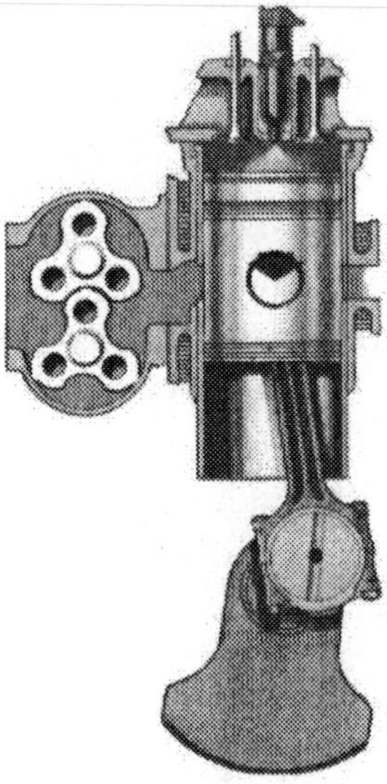

STROKE 2
POWER

Courtesy Detroit Diesel
Figure 14

The moment of ignition.

Since there is a full charge of air in the cylinder and enough temperature to ignite the small amount of incoming fuel we have set ourselves up for a seeming disaster. Lots of air and a lean mixture should produce a very rapid burn, perhaps even a detonation. Remember that clak-alak-alak that you hear emanate from the engine. That is detonation in anybody's language.

Is it destructive? Not at all. Why should the diesel run in detonation without damage? In a word-- design. The diesel engine is built quite heavily and uniquely designed to accept this situation.

The speed at idle is very slow and there is no load upon the engine. The combustion chamber is an open vortex in the piston head facing upward and it is within this vortex that the explosion occurs. Because of this the force of that explosion is itself directed upward at the flat surface of the cylinder head.

This protects the cylinder walls from the effects of detonation. Perhaps most importantly, there is only a small amount of fuel needed to maintain an idle speed. The explosion is uncontrolled, and the burn rate is excessively fast, but the amount of energy developed is limited by that small amount of fuel admitted to the cylinder. Thus no damage occurs to the engine.

Let us proceed to the next phase. We begin to open the throttle and add greater amounts of fuel to the process. The injector directs the plume of fuel at carefully controlled areas of the combustion chamber. Now the shape of that chamber becomes very important.

There are many different shapes for the combustion chamber of the diesel engine but most of them share a few common attributes. Consider the top of the piston. On the diesel engine, the piston has a greater height above the wrist pin than that of a gasoline engine. This provides room for the combustion chamber.

The piston top is machined into a vortex shape which may incorporate a bowl or partial sphere for its basis. In the center of this bowl there is a small cone shaped protrusion facing upward with the point of the cone towards the piston top. When the injector plume is sprayed onto this point it is met with a loop shaped structure in every direction or at any point around the cone.

The fuel is encouraged to mix smoothly and evenly

with the heated air and to burn at an even rate across the cylinder. Gone is the previous problem of detonation. The engine now runs smoothly. The flame propagates steadily across the cylinder and the engine gets an even push to the piston top.

Sounds great. What are the possible pitfalls? Begin with pre-ignition. This can be a very real problem for the diesel. This condition is caused when an injector leaks and a few drops of fuel are made available to the cylinder before the proper time. The engine now fires early with the piston on the way up and tries to run backwards.

Pressure from the burning fuel is trying to push the piston back the wrong way and under certain conditions this effort may be great enough to bend a connecting rod, or worse.

Pre-ignition is a definite threat to the health of your diesel.

Then there is the matter of excess fuel, an overly rich mixture. This usually occurs when the mechanic has installed a set of oversized injectors into an engine in an effort to get more horsepower. The diesel cannot burn this excess fuel. There is simply not enough air present within the cylinder to cleanly burn the fuel. The smoke in your exhaust will aggravate and accumulate but even worse is the possibility that the excess fuel will wash down the cylinders. When this occurs the lubricating oil is washed off the cylinder walls and galling is inevitable. This calls for a complete overhaul in most cases.

Given the proper amount of fuel to balance the available amount of air and delivered at the proper moment, the diesel will thrive. We know the diesel does not get all of the fuel that it is to receive from the injector into the cylinder immediately. Rather the fuel is delivered in a prolonged spray of measured duration.

Under these conditions the engine is going to have, for a brief moment, the same conditions in the cylinder at operating speed that it did at idle. There will be a small amount of fuel with a large amount of air. This condition leads to detonation at idle speed. Why should it not do so at operating speed?

In a word, it does. The result is actually a kind of mini-detonation. We call it a spike.

Think about a pressure curve on which we plot the pressures in the engine cylinder over a complete revolution. Begin with the initial pressure of the open cylinder; pass through the act of compression and through the power stroke.

That graph would climb slowly until the fuel ignites in the cylinder. When the first fuel hits the cylinder the pressure will spike upward sharply but taper off rapidly. This spike occurs so quickly and lasts for such a short time that no damage is done.

There are all manners of injector delivery patterns designed to work with this problem. Each has some benefits and each has its drawbacks. There are shapes and arrangements within the individual combustion chambers to counteract the effects of the spike. Some of these are more effective than others.

In the end it becomes evident some small spike is to be expected and is not a matter for concern. It is only when that spike becomes prolonged and more intense that it becomes a matter of utmost gravity. Given any encouragement, that spike can become destructive.

The twin problems of spikes and detonation are of greatest concern on those engines with turbochargers. The greater the boost on the engine, the greater is the potential for damage. That turbocharger provides additional air to the engine cylinder. Lots and lots of additional air is present at every revolution.

That additional air requires additional fuel to damp the burn rate, keep the pressures even and cool the engine. So long as there is plenty of fuel to keep the pressure even and the burn rate under control, the engine is happy. If the mixture begins to lean out, even a little bit, the turbocharged engine will do something ugly to your pocket book.

I do not want to belabor the point but I do want to mention two things. First, you must keep the fuel filters clean, the injectors in top operating condition and every bit of the fuel delivery system working properly if your high boost turbo engine is expected to live. Second, remember that admonition from the chapter on engine selection when I suggested that you consider only the continuous duty horsepower available from a given power plant? Let me expand upon that just a bit. Last week I got a brochure advertising a well-known diesel engine for sale. The engine turned 3,800 RPMs, maximum speed and developed an advertised 231 horsepower (approximately). The continuous RPM rating was at 3,600 RPMs and at those speeds there was about 181 horsepower available. What does this tell me? Remember the elements of horsepower.

If we keep the same cubic displacement in the engine and turn the same number of RPMs, there is only one place to get more horsepower and that is through added cylinder pressure. Here we have an increase of 2,000 RPMs (3,600 to 3,800) or about 0.5 percent increase. Yet the horsepower rose nearly 28 percent within that same RPM change.

How can that happen? Pressure, and more pressure. When you see this situation with lots of horsepower tacked onto the end of the RPM curve you are seeing lots of boost added to the mix. You may still want this engine for a particular installation but BE CAREFUL. Be careful when you buy, be careful when you install, and be careful how you maintain.

The spikes in that boost pressure do not guarantee spikes in the cylinder pressure or an early demise for the engine itself, but they do make the mariner think about flame propagation and the lessons of detonation.

CHAPTER FIFTEEN
THE FOUR QUADRANTS

This chapter is intended to pursue relationships in the engine. You will have to read this carefully because it is going to introduce a concept I have not seen in print before. We are going to divide crankshaft travel into four quadrants and use this division to show changing relationships that are interesting to say the least.

There is no mystery about the principles involved but you will get a different view of the functions of the engine from this chapter. Read it carefully and try to recognize the elements of those relationships.

First, I want you to think about the arm on the crankshaft. That arm rotates and the rod journal describes a complete circle for each revolution. You are now looking at the crankshaft from the timing gear end of the engine.

As the engine rotates the crankshaft will describe a 360-degree circle. Divide that circle into 4 quadrants. The first line will run from top to bottom, passing through the top dead center and bottom dead center positions on the crankshaft.

The second line will pass across the circle at right angles to the first line, making a 90-degree mark and a 270-degree mark away from that first vertical line. We now have the circle divided into four points at 0, 90, 180, and 270 degrees.

First let us discuss the significance of each of these marks. At 0 we have the beginning of all events in the crankshaft cycle. That is significant also because all timing of the engine begins here. The camshaft, valve action, and injector timing all relate to this mark.

The 180 degree mark is at bottom dead center, the 90 degree mark is exactly perpendicular to the center line on the right side, and the 180 degree mark is perpendicular to the center line on the left side.

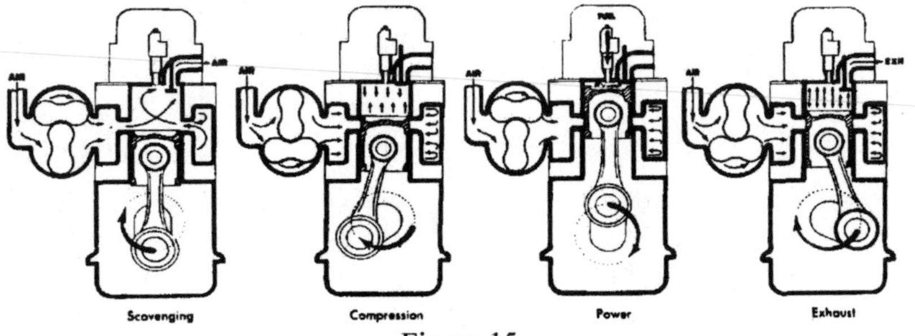

Figure 15

The four quadrants.

Visualize the crankshaft as it passes over that 0 or top dead center mark. The crankshaft arm is almost straight up and any pressure exerted upon the piston is pushing straight downward, with no developed torque. In fact, pressure at this time is wasted, even though it is inevitable.

We call this dead travel in the crankshaft and this is a well-documented fact. It lasts for about 5 crankshaft degrees, 2-1/2 degrees on each side of the 0 mark. The next considerations have not had so much press.

As the crankshaft continues to rotate the angle on the arm increases and the developed torque begins to rise. Pressure on the arm is being translated into twisting movement and this is being translated into rotation.

Follow this closely: as the crankshaft descends, the angle will become ever greater until the shaft reaches 90 degrees from the vertical. The faster this angle changes the faster the piston moves in an ever-increasing relationship.

Thus we have a piston whose speed of movement, measured in thousandths of an inch, increases for every degree the crankshaft turns. This in the first quadrant.

In the second quadrant, the piston moves less and less for every degree the crankshaft turns. As the piston approaches bottom dead center, the reverse of the above situation takes place. The angle between crankshaft and piston is now decreasing and soon they will be in a straight line, relative to each other.

In the third quadrant the piston is now past bottom dead center and rising. Again, we had a 5-degree dead space at bottom dead center during which the piston did not move with the crankshaft. Now, in the third quadrant, the piston moves at an increasing speed, relative to the degrees of crankshaft travel. The angle between piston and crankshaft is growing.

This continues until the crankshaft reaches the 270-degree mark and the situation reverses itself. From here, the crankshaft is approaching the 0 mark again and the relationship between crankshaft travel in degrees and piston movement in thousandths of an inch has a decreasing component.

Thus we see that in quadrants 1 and 3 the relationship between crankshaft movement and piston travel have an increasing relationship. The piston will move an ever-greater distance for each degree of crankshaft travel all the way across the first and third quadrants.

In quadrants two and four, the relationship reverses itself. The piston travel pursues an ever-decreasing relationship. The piston travel in thousandths of an inch becomes less and less for every degree of crankshaft rotation.

Why is this relationship important? Well, those dead areas are certainly significant since not much is happening at this point and we have to make allowance for this in timing, intake systems and other areas.

How about camshaft design? The amount of air/fuel mix that the engine demands changes at an ever-increasing rate as the piston travels downward in that first quadrant. Valve openings and flow characteristics must recognize this need: an ever changing need like a moving target.

Think about the calculations involved. What the volume of the cylinder is at any given spot in the crankshaft travel. How fast the engine is turning. How fast the piston will move for the next degree of crankshaft travel. What the volume of the cylinder will be after the piston moves for that single degree of crankshaft travel. The difference between these two figures can be translated into demand for air/fuel mix at a given speed.

Now address the valve sizes, camshaft lift, manifold diameters, venturi diameter and jet sizes. This just to estimate flow for a single degree of crankshaft travel. That is on the intake stroke alone. On the power stroke we see another problem.

Pressure from the burning charge is greatest at top dead center when the crankshaft arm is nearly vertical and makes the least torque. As the crankshaft continues to rotate, the cylinder pressure is falling. That single charge of air/fuel mix that burnt in the cylinder is actually losing pressure.

The crankshaft arm however is becoming more effective as it turns. The engine will have an ever-increasing potential to produce torque as the crankshaft approaches 90 degrees. The angle between piston and crankshaft arm will be best for the production of torque as pressure on the piston is running out.

The next consideration is piston travel and rod angularity. The piston moves in a straight line, up and down. The wrist pin follows that line. The angle between the line of piston travel and the connecting rod journal on the crankshaft is called rod angularity.

The more acute this angle becomes, the less pressure is transferred from the piston to the crankshaft. The less acute or the straighter is this angle, the more pressure is transferred. It becomes obvious a short rod will produce a very acute angle with less torque.

A long rod will produce a much straighter angle with

greater pressure transfer and more torque produced. The problem is easy to see. A long rod will require the engine block be deeper and heavier. The long rod will be easier to bend but it is more efficient.

The short rod will produce less torque for a unit of pressure but the block can be lower and lighter. The short rod is stiffer and less likely to bend or break. Also the short rod with its lighter loading tends to wrap up (accelerate) faster than the long rod.

What are we to do? Save iron, add acceleration, and keep the rod short or increase the deck height of the block, add more iron, and increase both torque and efficiency? This is an ongoing argument among engine builders.

In the world of high performance engines where people tailor the crankshaft/rod assembly to specific needs the stroke of the engine and the length of the rod are shuffled continuously for different applications. The man who shuffles best wins.

The dead travel, inertia and rod angle losses, are all detailed here and have an adverse effect on engine performance. We know these ills exist but we do not know how to cure them.

In fact, no one has ever been able to solve these problems in an internal combustion engine. They are problems that cause serious energy losses in the engine and contribute to the dismal efficiency numbers with which we are faced. Just how much energy do we really lose in the change from fuel to horsepower? This is a shocker.

The very best of our gasoline engines is about 19 percent to 20 percent efficient. Yes, we waste roughly 80 percent of our gasoline in the effort to convert fuel to useable power and I do not mean this in the sense of atomic conversion.

Using the BTUs of heat energy in a gallon of gasoline versus the horsepower produced by burning it in an engine gives a figure that we call, thermal efficiency. That figure yields a fraction less than 1/5th. We lose 4 gallons of gasoline out of every 5 that we burn in the engine.

This is a terrible waste and sure, there must be a better way but thus far it has not emerged.

Where does all that fuel go? That is a considerable part of the exercise we have just finished. Remember those starts and stops at top dead center and bottom dead center? That is where the kinetic losses occur.

The dead travel at top dead center absorbs a good deal of our fuel. And that slowly changing angle between piston and crankshaft arm keeps torque production at a minimum while the strongest pressure from the burning fuel is being lost. But there is much more.

An enormous amount of fuel goes to cooling losses. Cooling losses occur when we circulate water or coolant through the engine. This absorbs many thousands of BTU's of heat energy and it wastes large quantities of fuel. Of course, we have no choice but to cool the engine or it would be destroyed.

The friction losses from bearings, piston rings and gears are substantial. The accessories we drive, 4 horsepower to drive the oil pump, twelve horsepower for a camshaft, all of these things require a portion of that fuel we burn.

Regardless of the many negatives that occur, the engine is still a marvel of engineering and it is a source of great pleasure to many sailors. It also does a lot of commercial work and no one can estimate how many steps or lifts it has spared mankind.

If you can think of a better way you will be remembered throughout history but otherwise we will have to struggle along with what we have.

CHAPTER SIXTEEN
DIESEL ENGINE DESIGN

There is a great deal of thought that goes into the design of a diesel engine. Much of the work today is done by a computer but that computer is simply reacting to a program written by people who first performed by physical means, each of the functions which the computer performs electronically.

Make no mistake about it, the knowledge programmed into that electronic marvel was paid for in sweat and tears. I cannot make you an engineer in one easy lesson but I do intend to give you a few pages of introduction to engine design.

What is contained here will help you to choose an engine for your vessel and to understand the engine another man has chosen. You should easily recognize whether he chose wisely or not and be better able to discuss the reason for those conclusions.

The purpose of the diesel engine is to produce horsepower and the designer works toward that end. We want as much horsepower as we can get from any given sized power plant with the greatest possible longevity and the lowest possible maintenance.

Naturally, we would like to consume as little fuel as possible while we develop this horsepower. For any given application we may be willing to juggle some of the design parameters to get a specific result, even if there is a cost somewhere else. First let us describe those parameters and then see how they may be juggled.

I would like to use Pal again for an example. Remember we have 4 inches of bore and 5 inches of stroke. This gives us an under square engine with 502.4 cubic inches of piston displacement from eight cylinders. For our purposes, let us assume that our efforts at engine design specify a given size for the engine and that 502 cubic inches is the limit.

What have we learned about the engine previously? Begin with the bore size, we know the diameter of the bore decides how much room we have for valves in the head. The valve size decides in turn, how much air we can get into the cylinder. The amount of air decides how much fuel we can burn and how much cylinder pressure we can create. The amount of cylinder pressure decides how many total pounds of pressure we can get on the piston top. We want all the cylinder pressure that we can get.

Here are the choices.

Option 1. A larger bore and reduce the length of the stroke. You will increase total pressure on the piston top. Now you can turn the engine higher with the same piston speeds and reduced kinetics.

Option 2. Reduce the bore and lose a bit of total pressure on the piston top. Increase the length of the stroke a bit to maintain our displacement figures and increase the low-end torque as well. We will up the piston speeds by doing so and increase the kinetics but that may be acceptable.

Option 3. Leave the engine as it is. The four-inch bore and 5 inch stroke we gave our Pal is fairly conservative for a diesel engine and the truth is any one of the above options may be reasonable.

How do we know what Pal is best suited to do in its present condition and which way to go for any future changes? Go to the bore/stroke ratio for the best clue. Pal has a bore/stroke ratio above one (1). It is presently under square and the actual figure is 1.250. The stroke is 25 percent greater than the bore.

This really is a conservative figure for a diesel but it still shows an imbalance towards a stroke that is all ready greater than the bore. Could we still stretch the arm on the crankshaft if we really wanted even more low end? Sure we can. Look at the second clue, piston speed. It is still low enough to accept a bit of an increase.

Just remember what the tradeoffs will be. If we really wanted to turn the engine a bit higher, could we reasonably increase the bore size? Sure we can. An increase in the Bore size would entail a shorter crankshaft arm and the power curve would come on later in the RPM range, but we already have a bit of an undersquare configuration.

I am not about to tell you what decisions to make. That is not my purpose. You are the engineer now and I want you to think about what your answer would be. Do you like Pal as it is or are you going to alter it and put your own stamp upon it?

I am going to briefly review the rules. First, engines with a bore size greater than the stroke will have good high RPM characteristics. It will build good pressure on those many square inches of piston surface but it will suffer on the bottom end. On the other hand, small-bore engines do not breathe as well and they get less pressure on the reduced number of square inches of piston surface.

A long stroke engine, an engine with a stroke size greater than the bore, will pull hard on the bottom end and develop good torque figures but will tend to fade as RPMs increase.

The terrible loads generated by kinetics can impose an unacceptable loss of power at high piston speeds.

There are a great many tradeoffs but what you are really looking at is the balance between those torque-at-RPM figures that are the basis for horsepower. How do I balance the numbers for the best performance and what, in my opinion is the best performance?

If you get these few principles down pat you will still not even be close to the information needed to design an engine but you will have some idea of what the designer had in mind when the engine was born. You will be better able to understand the engine you are looking at and decide, "Is this for me?"

You will also be able to decide if the engine someone else bought is going to do the job for which they bought it. We have discussed the tradeoffs that the designer faces. Now let us look at the numerical limits that tell us specific things about our engine design.

Look at the bore/stroke ratio. (Divide the bore into the stroke). Engines with a number below one (1) are RPM engines. They have to turn higher RPMs to get a given horsepower. Engines with a number above one (1) are torque engines. They pull on the bottom end. Our Pal is a torque engine with a bore/stroke ratio of 1.250.

Horsepower-per-cubic-inch is a great indicator. An engine with one horsepower or more for each cubic inch will not generally last more than 2,000 hours, if you use the horsepower. Engines with more than two cubic inches per horsepower will generally run 10, 000 hours or more before overhaul.

Engines with three or more cubic inches per horsepower may run 15,000 to 20,000 hours between majors. These are simply personal parameters I have established during 40 years of observation. They are not backed by scientific study and they were not conducted in a laboratory.

If you are told that some Super Gizmo engine will get a great deal better performance than shown above, you may want to take the information with a grain of salt. Select from the boaters that you know, pick a category among the engines outlined above, and see how many engines you can find that have done appreciably better.

How does our Pal stack up in its present form? With a 5-inch stroke we can turn the engine 3,000 RPMs and the piston speed will still be below 2,500 feet per minute. A cruising speed of 2400 RPMs will place the piston speed at just below 2,000 feet per minute. Good numbers.

Using a 3,000 RPM red line (top RPMs) and a 2,400 RPM cruise puts Pal in the Light Duty engine category. Many manufacturers would disagree but it is a proper designation. True heavy-duty diesels are indeed very large and very heavy.

This engine should develop about 200 horsepower at full throttle or 3,000 RPMs. It should also produce about 160 horsepower at the cruising speed of 2,400 RPMs. Our pal has 502 cubic inches, thus we have one horsepower for each 2.51 cubic inches, at top speed. Even at maximum RPMs. This is still a fairly conservative figure. Pal should go quite a while.

Should we look at a turbo charged version of this engine? If we are going to design a higher horsepower version of Pal do we want to increase the RPMs a bit so that less boost will be required for a given horsepower or go for turbo boost alone to get the job done? What do we know?

We know Pal has very conservative piston speeds. We know it can handle an increase in RPMs. We also know pressure creates heat. High turbo pressures CAN create excessive heat. Here is another potential tradeoff. Raise the RPMs and raise the piston speeds or keep the low RPM performance and raise the boost pressure to get the desired horsepower.

Let me offer a suggestion. If you are going to use small to moderate boost, why not hold those low RPM figures and keep the lower piston speeds. You will also keep the smaller kinetics. On the other hand, if you are going for higher horsepower figures, why not raise the RPMs a bit and reduce the amount of boost needed to get that horsepower?

Now we do not have to have cylinder pressures so high that we are skirting the edge of disaster. How about weight? That is an important figure that has dropped through the cracks, thus far. Weight is very important for several reasons.

We know engines with a low power-to-weight ratio are likely to have greater structural strength than are those with higher power to weight ratios. If we are looking at two engines of like horsepower, the heavier engine MAY last longer but MAY also be too heavy for your vessel.

The tradeoffs that were made during engine design are rather apparent as you observe the finished engine. You should now be better able to see the result of these decisions which others have made when they designed their engines and you should be better able to choose.

Look at the engine on paper. How many cubic inches? How much bore and how much stroke? What is the bore/stroke ratio? If the engine is turbo charged, how much boost? You should be able to get into the head of the designer. You should understand where he placed the emphasis. The elements of horsepower are all centered around cubic displacement, cylinder pressure, and RPMs.

These are the basic tools the designer must work with. You must look at the balance and see the tradeoffs. Then make your decisions based upon that information. There is one further piece of intelligence that is important in the decisions you will make. That is the matter of gears and transmissions.

Parts of this chapter are a bit redundant but it is important to see the principles involved in as many ways as you possibly can. See the same subject from every angle and the answers will become more easily recognized as the questions appear.

What we have not yet explored is the matter of bearing areas (square inches of bearing surface at rod and main journals) and other similar indicators of engine life. There are simply too many potentials to view them all but we have certainly covered those you can assimilate quickly.

In the next chapter we will focus on the manner gears relate to torque, horsepower, and the RPMs. That is a fascinating game and one which few mariners or mechanics really seem to understand.

I hope you will thoroughly assimilate this chapter and then learn to make the vital connections between the engine design and the gear train. A combination of the two is required to really tailor the engine package to the job.

Figure 16
Courtesy of Yanmar

Figure 16a
Courtesy of Yanmar

Figure 16b
Courtesy of Yanmar

Figure 16c
Courtesy of Yanmar

Figure 16d
Courtesy of Balmar

The four Yanmar engines above are all designed for different applications aboard various vessels. The last engine is a Balmar, designed for stationary work. This engine drives an alternator, water maker and generator.

CHAPTER SEVENTEEN
GEARS & TRANSMISSIONS

In this chapter we will explore the subject of transmissions and gear trains. I want to begin with the transmissions themselves and consider the hardware involved. Afterward we will move on to the subject of effect. How does the gear and the selection thereof relate to the work it must do? I will answer that question as well. As we explore the many features and operations of the marine transmission you will quickly realize there are several types of transmissions and numerous things to remember about each. You must concentrate upon the descriptions in this chapter in order to recognize each of the permutations we will describe.

The transmission for the marine engine transmits power from the engine to the propeller shaft. It requires an input shaft to accept power from the engine and an output shaft to deliver power to the propeller shaft.

Within the transmission there must be some provision for direction change so Forward-Neutral-Reverse direction movements can be accomplished. Some type of clutch assembly generally provides this direction change. Besides the direction change, the transmission may also provide some type of change in the speed of the shafts.

There are three possibilities.

1. The input shaft and the output shaft may turn at exactly the same RPMs.

When the input RPMs are the same as the output RPMs on any transmission it is said to have a 1:1 ratio. In this instance the transmission is sometimes described as a clutch. This is because there is no speed increase or reduction within the unit.

Figure 17
Courtesy of Borg Warner

Typical marine gear.

2. The input shaft may turn more RPMs than the output shaft.

This system is commonly called a reduction gear because the output RPMs are reduced in relation to the input RPMs. The mathematical expression of this relationship is called the gear ratio. When it is written, the gear ratio always has the RPMs of the input shaft first and it may look like this 1.5: 1.

In this model we see the input shaft must turn 1.5 times for each revolution of the output shaft. The reduction gear is sometimes described as an under driven gear because the output shaft RPMs are always under the input shaft RPMs.

3. The input shaft may turn fewer RPMs than the output shaft. These relationships are described as the gear ratio.

The very presence of an under-driven gear suggests the possibility of an overdriven gear and, of course, there are many such gears in use. The overdrive gear produces more RPMs at the output shaft than those it receives from the input shaft. Again, the mathematical expression of that relationship is called the gear ratio.

As before, when it is written the RPMs of the input shaft appear first and the model may look like this 1:1.5. In this model we should understand that for every revolution we provide to the input shaft, the output shaft will respond with 1.5 revolutions.

SHAFT ALIGNMENT

Besides the gear ratio there are several possible configurations for the shaft alignment on any transmission. The input shaft may be on the same line or axis as the output shaft and in this situation the transmission is said to be coaxial. The output shaft may appear below the input shaft and this transmission is considered to be a drop center gear.

Further, there are gears that have the output shaft on a down angle in relationship to the axis of the input shaft. The purpose of this gear is to permit the engine to be mounted level or more nearly level. Down angle gears come with varying amounts of angle and usually run between 8.0 and 12.0 degrees.

ROTATION

Besides gear ratio and shaft configuration, the transmission has several potential rotational arrangements. The input shaft and the output shaft turn in the same direction. This is the normal or standard system. The input shaft and the output shaft turn in opposite directions. This transmission is referred to as a reversing gear.

There are transmissions that can be made to perform in either manner. They may provide normal operation or reverse the direction of the output shaft. I want to offer a word of caution about this condition. Some of those transmissions, which can be reversed, may not perform very well in the reverse mode.

Always consult the manufacturer recommendations before adjusting any transmission for reverse operation. There are many aspects of gear train design, which do not appear on the surface, nor do they necessarily manifest themselves immediately if you violate the manufacturer directions.

Be assured the liberties taken with your transmission may well come back to haunt you. The least of your problems will be a voided transmission warranty. No manufacturer will honor the warranty on a transmission that has been rotated in the wrong direction, under load.

IN GENERAL

If you find the above descriptions difficult to follow at least remember these things in selecting a transmission: 1. Gear ratio, 2. Direction of rotation for the input shaft, 3. Direction of rotation of the output shaft 4. Angle of the output shaft, 5 maybe most important of all remember what you hope to accomplish and try to be certain your selection accomplishes your goals.

WHY A REDUCTION GEAR?

We have covered the general features of the transmission and its operation. Besides providing for the forward-neutral-reverse accommodation, what does the transmission do for me? Why do I want a gear train?

Early on in this book I described the relationship between torque and horsepower and to explain the principles which govern each. Horsepower is torque, as it moves through a unit of time. In this Chapter we will explore the relationship between them and the element of time which binds them together.

First, let us again state the nature of torque. Torque is a potential. It is measured in foot-pounds. A one pound force, applied to a lever one foot in length, at a distance of 1 foot from the centerline of a shaft will produce one foot pound of torque. The value of this unit of torque is written as 1 lbs./ft.

As stated previously, torque does not move. It has no ability to do work. As soon as torque begins to move against a load it is measurable as horsepower. Horsepower is capable of doing work. It is measured in terms of actual work it can accomplish in one minute. The amount of work is placed at 33,000 lbs./ft. Notice the elements: a unit of work and a time in which it is to be accomplished.

How does this relate to the gear train? The gear train changes the rate work is done. It cannot add horsepower but it can add or subtract torque by changing the rate it is delivered.

As an example. Begin with an engine that develops one (1) horsepower. It will lift 33,000 pounds, one foot, in one minute. It will also lift 16,500 pounds, two feet, in one minute or 66,000 pounds a half foot, in one minute. The rate at which the work is delivered is changing in each example. What is not changing is the total amount of work that is accomplished. In each example we performed 33,000 foot pounds of total work, in one minute. To lift that 66,000 pound load we had to slow the rate of delivery. That is what the reduction gear does. To lift that 16,500 pound load an extra foot, in the same time frame, we had to speed the rate of delivery. This is what an overdrive gear does. Neither system effects the total amount of work accomplished or the horsepower of an engine but it sure can change the delivered torque. In fact, it can make drastic changes either upward or downward, in the delivered torque of the engine.

As an example. An engine delivers 200 lbs./ft. of torque at 3000 RPMs.

Using the formula we learned earlier in this book we see that 200 x 3,000 divided by 5252 equals 114.24 horsepower. Let us run this through a 2:1 reduction gear.

We know the shaft RPMs will be halved to just 1,500 RPMs. Will we lose horsepower? No. The torque will be doubled at the output shaft in direct proportion to the reduction in RPMs. Now try 400 lbs./ft. of torque x 1,500 RPMs and divide by 5252. We still have exactly 114.24 horsepower.

How about the overdrive gear? It would produce the same result, in reverse. Output RPMs would be doubled and torque reduced by half but the horsepower would remain unchanged. This is not a mathematical gimmick. It is exactly what happens when horsepower is applied to a gear train.

What value is the reduction gear or the overdrive gear? The reduction gear allows us to pull a larger propeller with the same amount of horsepower. We cannot pull that larger propeller at the same RPMs as a smaller one but we can reduce the slip from the small blade and tow greater loads.

The overdrive gear allows us to increase the RPMs at the propeller and turn it much faster, if top end speed is the object. This system is used on many racing vessels and Unlimited Hydroplanes utilized overdrive gears for many years.

What the diesel mechanic or boat owner needs to know is this:

1. I can increase torque with a gear train but not horsepower.

2. Any engine can be tailored to the required job, some better than others, by using a gear train.

3. By understanding the above illustrations it is possible to do a much better job of selecting an engine and transmission package which will be satisfactory in the vessel.

High revving engines in motorcycles and high performance sports cars develop quantities of low-end torque through the use of a gear train. In fact, those types of vehicles may have five, six, or even seven different gear ratios to multiply the available torque at any given RPMs. The mariner has but one fixed gear ratio. Thus the wide set of options are not available to him but limited changes can be orchestrated by a given engine/transmission combination.

The next chapter will cover propeller performance and selection. Afterward we will take a look at the entire drive train, engine, gear, and propeller as a unit. You have the first two steps in the selection process set forth in the Engine Design and Transmission Chapters. Now let us move on to the final part of the driveline, the propeller.

CHAPTER EIGHTEEN
PROPELLERS DESIGN & SELECTION

When it comes to vessel performance, propellers are a very fertile field to plow. No boat of any type will perform its best without a propeller to match the engine and transmission. I will tell you first about the features and design of propellers and then we will move on to selection.

Propellers are measure by their diameter and pitch. The diameter is the circle that will be described by the outside tips of the blades during any revolution. The dimension of that circle will be given in inches.

The pitch of a propeller is described as the distance the propeller will travel in a single revolution, if there were no slip. It is always given in inches, not degrees and it is less certain in its measurement than is the diameter.

Why not degrees and why so uncertain? Modern propellers have a variable pitch with a different amount of pitch at the hub than at the tips of the blades. This change or twist varies in degrees and the blade would be different at any point of measure. The rate of this change is referred to as the rate of twist and it can be vastly different from manufacturer to manufacturer.

For this reason, among others, propellers may also vary in performance from manufacturer to manufacturer. This disparity is seen in outboard propellers to a greater degree than inboard propellers but the difference remains.

What I really want you to understand from this is the fact two propellers of like dimension from two different manufacturers MAY perform differently. Even though they are given the same dimensions on their specification sheet. So we come to Fleming's First Law for Propeller Selection, "Propeller pitch is more important for comparison purposes than for absolute dimension."

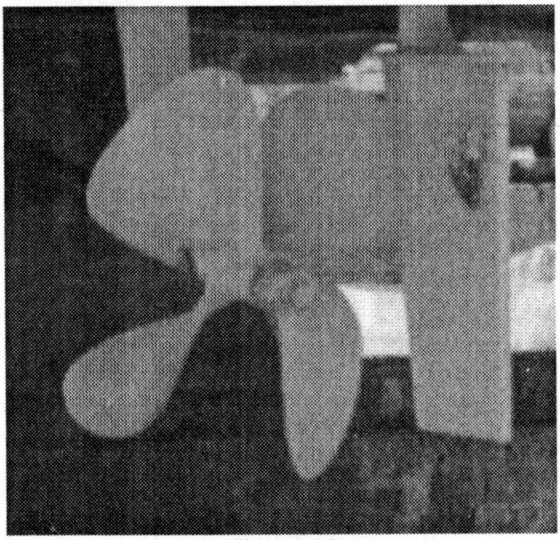

Figure 18
Courtesy of John P. Kaufman

Typical propeller for a planning hull.

The propeller has a hub at the center of the propeller itself. The hub is bored on a taper or angle with standard dimensions. It has a keyway or slot milled into one side and running the length of the hub. This keyway is mated to the propeller shaft with a metal key.

The key itself is an elongated strip of square stock that will not usually shear under load. The inboard propeller does not routinely employ any type of protection against impact. Thus any collision between the propeller and a solid object may have disastrous results.

The propeller may have two blades, or more, but

seldom more than six. The blades emanate as radials from the hub and the surface area is measured in square inches of surface. In bygone years these blades were referred to as flukes because of their resemblance to the flukes of a whale. The term is still used on occasion today.

Those features of the propeller we will look at most closely are the ones described above; diameter, pitch, and blade area. The real effects of the variation in twist rate from brand to brand can only be felt by testing the propeller on your vessel.

Propellers with identical dimensions for diameter and pitch are said to be square and they are balanced. Propellers with a diameter greater than the pitch are oversquare while those with a diameter which is less than the pitch are said to be undersquare.

Undersquare propellers tend to be for higher speeds. They have less blade area in relationship to their diameter and they will slip more under load. Yet, they also have a greater potential to move further for each rotation of the blade.

Oversquare propellers generally are used for mid range speeds while grossly oversquare propellers are designed for heavy loads. Additional blade area may reduce slip and that is the reason for those four and five blade propellers you sometimes see. Reduced slip may be a desirable effect on any vessel at any speed.

What propeller do I want for my vessel and how can I decide? There are several ways to approach this subject. Before we begin I would offer you Fleming's Second Law for Propeller Selection, "Load the engine with the propeller and drive the boat with the tachometer." What does it mean? I believe in the concept of a propeller as a governor. Set the high idle on your engine at 50 RPMs above factory recommended maximum and then load the engine with the propeller until it exactly drops into the factory numbers.

Two things you can believe. First, this is the only way to be certain that the propeller is really matched to the boat. Second, if the propeller is either too large or too small at the top end of the RPM range it will always be too large or too small throughout the entire RPM range.

Naturally aspirated engines do not like to be overloaded with excessive propeller dimensions. Turbo charged engines MUST NOT be overloaded with excessive propeller dimensions. The more boost you are running, the less tolerance the engine will have for excessive loads.

Now we come to Fleming's Third Law For Propeller Selection. "Use a propeller which attains full factory RPMs with the heaviest load you intend to tow or carry." If you use widely disparate loads and you employ a propeller with dimensions for the heaviest of these, you will obviously be able to run the engine up against the governor at will.

That is why our first law said, "Drive it with the tachometer." If you are propped for a heavy load which is not presently on the vessel you will lose some potential speed but that is the cost of towing or carrying heavy loads. Just watch the tachometer and keep the RPMs at cruise or below. This is better than overloading the engine while you are towing or carrying a load.

How do I know if I have the right propeller and whether it is doing the job properly? I am going to show you how to calculate propeller efficiency. There are calculators that do this for you and almost any good propeller shop can give you the figures from information you supply but it is worthwhile to understand the process anyway.

Begin with the engine RPMs of the Pal engine. Earlier we set the cruise RPMs at 2,400. Assume we are using a 2:1 gear and the output revolutions are 1,200. Let us try a propeller with 18 inches of pitch and convert inches to feet or fractions thereof.

We see that 18 inches, divided by twelve inches in one foot, equals 1.5 feet. Multiply by 1,200 turns in each minute and we get 1,800 feet per minute. Let us convert feet to miles. Divide 5,280 feet into 1,800 feet and we get 0.341 miles. This is miles per minute since we were operating on Revolutions Per Minute.

Let us then covert miles per minute to miles per hour. Multiply that 0.341 by 60 and we see that the POTENTIAL speed of the vessel is 20.46 miles per hour, assuming 100 percent efficiency. For the purpose of this illustration let us assume the vessel is actually going 17.5 miles per hour.

Now we divide 20.46 into 17.5 and we see our propeller is actually 0.855 percent efficient. This means the slip is just under 15 percent. In some cases this would be excellent while in others it would be unacceptable.

If the engine turns at full factory RPMs and if slip is at a normal or below normal amount for the type of vessel, you probably will gain nothing from a change. Remember this, "The propeller cannot make horsepower. It can only take full advantage of the horsepower which the engine produces."

Should you decide to repower or make substantial changes, try to remember all of those things you have learned. You can juggle the engine measurements, changing from a long stroke to a short one or vice versa. You will do this by the engine you select.

You can change the engine RPMs at which it performs best by either changing engine dimensions (bore and stroke) or changing gear ratio.

You can change the amount of slip in your propeller by adding blade area, bigger diameter or a greater number of blades. You can make it possible to pull a bigger propeller with a change in gear ratio.

There are many things that go into the mating of parts in a drive train. You have had a minimal exposure to each of them. What you have learned here will not qualify you as an expert, but if you have truly assimilated the material, it will serve you in good stead.

What I want you to do is to think about the boats you have owned before and those you have seen as an observer. Consider those propeller situations you see in the future, all in the light of what is written on these pages. Then you will sec the principles play themselves out in the real world and experience will make the knowledge yours.

If you own a boat with a small diameter propeller and a real steering problem, maybe it needs a reduction gear and a bigger propeller. Is there room under the vessel for the larger prop? Will the strut clear? How will the larger propeller effect performance of the vessel? More or less speed? Better fuel economy or more consumption?

You are now the technician. It is your decision.

CHAPTER NINETEEN
GRAPHS AND CURVES

The engine manufacturer provides a set of engine specifications that are very useful to the mechanic or boat owner. They are contained in the torque curves, horsepower curves, and fuel consumption curves. There are others but these are the ones of greatest interest.

What do we learn from these graphic presentations of engine performance? First let us discuss what these curves are and then move on to their uses. The torque curve has an X and a Y axis with engine RPMs displayed along one axis and developed torque along the other.

The horsepower curve has an X and a Y axis with RPMs on one axis and horsepower on the other. The fuel curve also has an X and a Y axis with RPMs on one of those axes and fuel consumption on the other. Some manufacturers include two or more of these, torque, horsepower and fuel on the same graph.

I will develop the meanings of the different curves separately and then endeavor to show you the interconnected nature of all three. Let us begin with the torque curve.

As we look at the torque curve we will see that developed torque begins at the zero line and increases right along with the growing RPMs. This continues throughout the lower RPM ranges. As RPMs continue to increase however, the developed torque will finally reach a peak.

After this peak the RPMs continue to increase, but the developed torque begins to fall off.

At first, it will fall slowly but then as RPMs continue to rise, the drop in developed torque becomes quite rapid. This is the result of falling pressure on the piston top.

The induction system has also peaked and it can no longer fully satisfy the demand for air/fuel mix made by the cylinder. It cannot provide the energy to continue the rise in developed torque.

Now look at the horsepower curve. Beginning with the zero point, the horsepower will also increase as the RPMs increase. Yet eventually, it too peaks. Peak RPMs for the horsepower curve will always come at a higher point in the curve than will developed torque.

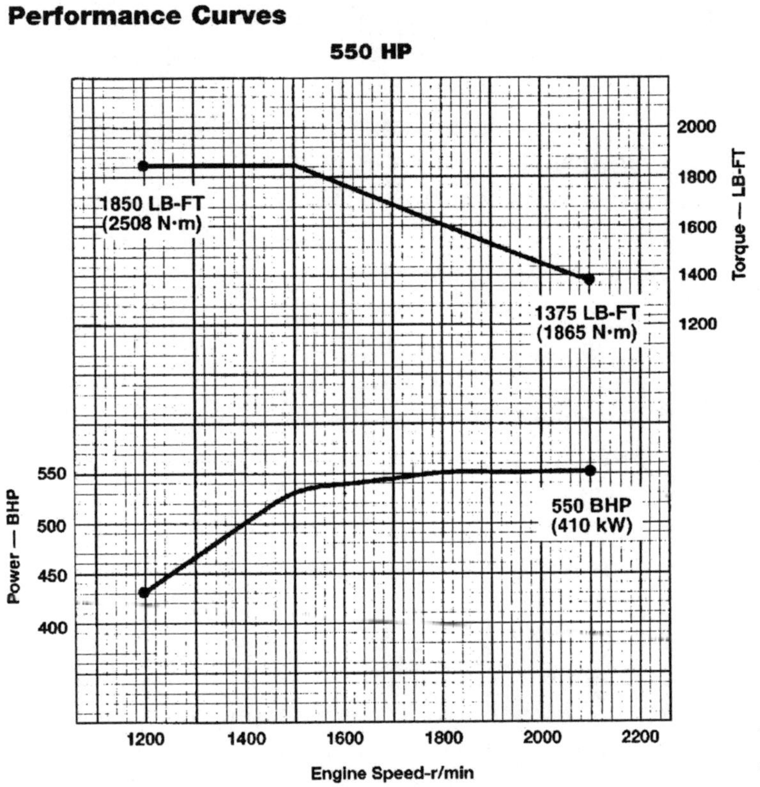

Courtesy Detroit Diesel
Figure 19

Why? The answer lies in the interconnected relationship between the two. Horsepower is a multiple of the factors, torque and RPMs. For a time, the RPMs will increase at a faster rate than the developed torque falls. Under these conditions, horsepower continues to increase.

This situation cannot continue indefinitely. Finally, as the induction system gets an ever-greater demand from the cylinder it will breathe out. Mean effective cylinder pressure becomes ever lower and torque falls off at a rate faster than the RPMs are increasing.

From this point on the horsepower too will begin to fall. For a short time horsepower will fall gradually, but then as RPMs become still higher, it will fall very rapidly.

For how many RPMs will the horsepower increase after torque begins to decline? This will depend upon engine design, the bore/stroke ratio, camshaft design, and other factors. What practical lesson can I learn from these curves?

You can deduce several things. Look at the torque curve and see where the torque peak occurs. This is the point of maximum efficiency for the engine. It will also represent your best cruising speed. Take the peak RPMs from the torque curve and move over to the horsepower curve.

Looking at the horsepower curve, see how much horsepower is available at the RPMs at which the torque curve peaked. This is your continuous operating range. The amount of horsepower found at this RPM is what you can expect from the engine on a day in day out basis.

You really are not often concerned with the advertised maximum horsepower figures since you can only use the engine at this speed for a short time. Yet there may come a day when you will have to use that full potential from the engine. When that emergency does arise, the highest point on the horsepower curve will be the maximum RPMs you should turn the engine. It will also be the maximum horsepower available to you. When you turn the engine beyond this point you are losing both horsepower and performance. You are overworking the engine, to no avail. In a word, "Don't do it."

Stay within the RPM range that provides maximum horsepower. Get all the power you can get and quit.

There is simply no benefit in winding the power plant to greater and greater speeds if there is no increase in horsepower to reward you for doing so. You will consume a great deal of fuel and lose Miles Per Gallon into the bargain.

What about the fuel curve? The fuel curve shows fuel consumed at each RPM increment. It tells us many things. You should try to have all three curves available when you begin to read. With these at hand, you are ready to balance the fuel consumption against the horsepower produced at any RPM. This allows you to fine-tune your engine operation for the very best performance. The engine will deliver a certain number of horsepower per gallon of fuel. Using fuel consumed and horsepower produced, you can calculate the best operating speed. This is easy to calculate. Simply divide gallons per hour into horsepower and you will get a figure we refer to as gallons per horsepower hour. The engineer generally uses pounds of fuel rather than gallons, but gallons will do nicely.

Consider gallons per horsepower hour as an efficiency rating, which it truly is. Estimate that number for each one hundred revolutions on the curve. If you have a flow meter it will be interesting to see how your figures compare with those compiled by the factory.

Factory figures are very close and if you vary from their numbers just a bit, that is acceptable but if you have any large discrepancies you may have a problem with the engine. You may be getting a wake up call.

There is a great deal of good information in these curves. Torque curves, horsepower curves, fuel consumption curves, all tell their own story. If you did not understand either mechanical or mathematical explanations above, at least understand the curves.

Know the torque rises and falls with the RPMs. Horsepower rises and falls with the RPMs, but at a different rate. Remember the engine is most efficient at the RPMs where the torque curve peaks.

Know the RPMs at which the torque curve peaks is also your continuous operating range and the point at which the horsepower curve peaks is the maximum horsepower available, regardless of how fast you turn the engine.

See how torque, horsepower, and RPMs effect or relate to fuel consumption and if you only master these things, you are well paid for reading this chapter.

We are going to do a section on high performance diesels. It will not be lengthy and it will be devoted principally to turbocharging but this is an ever-growing field and any serious treatise on the subject of diesel engines should not ignore the turbocharger.

Torque and horsepower curves for turbocharged engines are heavily skewed towards the top end of the RPM scale. You will easily see from these charts how the performance varies dramatically as pressure from the turbocharger commences and grows.

CHAPTER TWENTY
GASOLINE VERSUS DIESEL

In this chapter we are going to consider the attributes of diesel engines and gasoline engines. We will set them up side by side and see how they stack up. The answers may not be exactly what you think. At any point where figures are given they will represent those provided by the factory.

Since the purpose of this chapter is to compare gasoline engines with diesel engines we might first decide in what power or performance categories we could actually find comparisons. That is not as easy to do as you may believe.

Let us begin with an understanding of the terms we apply to diesel performance. Specifically, I would address the matter of Light, Medium, and Heavy-duty diesels. These categorical descriptions have been terribly misused by the advertisers. I shall become a bit presumptuous for a moment and assign a meaning to each of them.

HEAVY DUTY

I am going to begin with slow speed, heavy duty, and diesel engines. These are engines that develop maximum horsepower at 500 RPMs or less. They may weigh as much as 400 pounds per horsepower. That is heavy-duty. For this category, the diesel is the only engine since there are no slow speed, heavy duty, gasoline fueled engines available.

MEDIUM DUTY

Diesel engines that turn 1800 RPMs, or less. These engines will generally weigh about 15 pounds to 40 pounds per horsepower and develop about one horsepower for every 4 cubic inches to 6 cubic inches of piston displacement.

There are no gasoline-fueled engines available in this category today and so we eliminate this category from possible consideration. Diesel engines in this group would include sailboat auxiliaries and engines for commercial fishing vessels. These two categories, heavy-duty diesels and medium duty diesels are the exclusive province of the oil burners.

LIGHT DUTY

Light duty engines of 500 horsepower to over 1,000 horsepower that turn 5,000 RPMs or more are needed for sport boats and racing applications. They must be very light indeed. The diesel engine cannot make the weight for this category and, in fact, they are not seen in the go-fast boats. This category is the province of the gasoline engine.

We have now narrowed the field for comparison to a dramatic degree. The truth is, there is only a very narrow band in which to compare gasoline engines and diesel engines. If you think about it you will realize that light duty engines in the category between 60 horsepower and 400 horsepower is the limit of that band.

Thus the majority of our comparisons must be for engines of 400 horsepower and below in the light duty category. We are not quite through with our eliminations. Let us again separate the engines we would compare. There is little reason to compare gasoline engines to naturally aspirated diesels except in a broad general manner.

The diesel will be heavier for a given horsepower; it will turn fewer RPMs and use less fuel. It will provide many more hours of use before it requires an overhaul. The gasoline engine will cost less, give more horsepower for a given weight and more horsepower per cubic inch.

This is still not a real world competition because the two engines are designed for service in different vessels. Let us take a closer look at engines within this category anyway. Begin with two engines, one gasoline fueled, the other diesel fueled, both are naturally aspirated.

I will use the 6-354 Perkins diesel, which has 354 cubic inches of displacement, and see how it stacks up against a Merc Cruiser 350 cubic inch gasoline engine. The Perkins diesel has four cubic inches more piston displacement than the Merc Cruiser, gasoline powered engine, yet develops 42 lbs./ft. less torque and just half as much horsepower (130 for the Perkins vs. 260 for the Merc Cruiser).

If both engines are pulled at their individual cruising speeds, 1,800 RPMs for the diesel and about 3,200 RPMs for the gasoline engine, the diesel will generally outlast the gasoline-powered engine, many times. The expected life of that Perkins diesel may exceed 20,000 hours.

The Merc Cruiser engine will seldom manage more than 3,000 hours. Both numbers assume proper maintenance and operation. Operating RPMs, kinetics, and piston speeds have a great deal to do with longevity. The Perkins engine will easily turn 1,800 RPMs for many years. What if I dropped the Merc Cruiser to the same speed?

I have no real world figures for the Merc Cruiser 350 but I do for the Chevrolet 454. I saw one of those engines running on a generator with natural gas for power at the Chevrolet plant in Michigan. It was turning a governed 1,450 RPMs. The engine had 25,000 hours on the clock, without a breakdown.

Here you can easily see why there is no real world comparison between the slower speed, low horsepower diesel and the high speed, gasoline engine. They would not be called upon to serve in the same types of vessels and they would be required to operate at widely divergent speeds. We have eliminated another category for comparison.

Where then is the real competition? The real competition is between the lightweight, high speed, turbo charged, diesel and the naturally aspirated gasoline engine which powers so many general-purpose boats, principally those of 33 feet and below.

Figure 20
Courtesy of Detroit Diesel

Figure 21
Courtesy of Mercury Marine

How can we fairly compare a naturally aspirated, gasoline engine to a turbo charged diesel? The best approach is to use vessel performance as a measuring device. The best test of an engine's performance in a given vessel is the performance of the vessel itself and this may be the only fair way to compare a boosted engine to a naturally aspirated engine.

How will the engines fare in on water tests? If you change from gasoline to diesel or vice versa, you will get a very good indication of engine comparison IN A GIVEN VESSEL but be careful of the conclusions you draw. The vessel may respond with a scintillating change in performance and exciting new numbers.

If it does so, you have a successful installation and reason to be proud of your selection.

What you do not have is reason to draw too many broad conclusions about the performance of engines as a class from that particular example.

As an example. A well-known boating writer recently cited several examples of older gasoline engine to newer diesel engine conversions.

The older gasoline engines were naturals while the newer diesel engines were turbo charged. The power increased, and the fuel consumption improved considerably with those newer diesel engines. The installation was successful and the vessel owner was very pleased. What are the problems here?

The older gasoline engines were truly older, much older and no mention was made of trying to tune and retest them before the change. The writer drew some pretty broad conclusions about the comparative performance of gasoline and diesel engines by comparing worn out gasoline engines to brand new diesels.

How the engines really stack up is better illustrated in a side by side test, run on identical vessels. Several years ago a set of tests were run on a 33 foot Tiara Pursuit equipped with the Caterpillar 3208 turbo charged engines at 350 horsepower.

Identical tests were run at that same time on a sister

vessel with the Merc Cruiser 454 cubic inch engines at 350 horsepower. At top speed the Merc Cruiser gasoline engines were just 8 miles per hour faster than the Caterpillar diesels. Run at the same speed, with the diesels wide open and throttles on the gasoline engines reduced to match the speed of the diesel, the difference in fuel consumption was less than 30 per cent.

What have I proved? Two things, first I picked a vessel with a deep V design that did not react well to the weight of those 3208s. Second, if I was trying to prove a colleague wrong I found a niche situation with which to contradict. Neither example, his or mine, speaks fairly to the general performance of the engines involved but only to the particular engine and vessel combination.

My philosophy professor once said, "Beware of averages. If a man is standing with one foot on a hot stove and the other on a block of ice, on the average, he is comfortable." I ask you to beware of general statements about engines and their performance. They may be as misleading as averages.

So, I offer you Rule # 1 in the diesel/gasoline engine comparison, "If you can possibly find a running engine in a vessel identical to your own make your comparisons on the basis of performance in the vessel."

If we did decide to go to the dynamometer and the spec sheet, how would the gasoline engine compare to the diesel in this narrow grouping? The diesel with the assistance of high boost pressure will produce as much horsepower per cubic inch as a gasoline engine.

Why so much boost? The diesel piston is heavier than that of a gasoline engine and the stroke is usually longer for a given piston displacement. To keep the kinetics under control the diesel strives for high horsepower at low RPMs. If you are not going to turn the engine faster for added power, you must increase the cylinder pressure.

The lightweight diesel uses those high boost pressures to really load the cylinder. In this manner the diesel will produce more torque and develop full horsepower at lower

RPMs on less fuel than a gasoline engine. Many of the newer turbo charged diesels are making one (1) horsepower per cubic inch.

What are the problems then? The high boost diesel is expensive, it is sensitive, and it is running right on the edge. High cylinder pressures generally mean high temperatures. Modern engine design is able to cope with this to some extent. Combustion chamber design, intercoolers, and fuel coolers can help but that high boost turbo charger allows only a small margin for error.

You must keep plenty of cool air in the engine room. If the process of providing cool air requires noisy vents there is no choice. You must not overload the engine, even a little bit. Diesel engine warranties may REQUIRE that your engine room meet certain specifications at all times or the warranty MAY not be honored.

Diesel engines in this category had a fair share of problems in the mid 90's. Many of those problems have been worked out and the engines may last the average boater for a lifetime. The gasoline engine may well do the same thing. Actual figures show the average boater operates the engines two hundred hours or less, annually.

At this rate either engine, gasoline or diesel, may last a lifetime. Trying to compare the two engines in a fair and impartial manner is really difficult. Keep in mind the fact that almost everyone who makes comparisons has an agenda. They set out to prove something and, by golly, they will prove it. How accurate the figures may be and how well drawn the lines of comparison is another question.

As the diesel loses weight, the Electronically Fuel Injected (EFI), gasoline engine is becoming more fuel-efficient so you must be cautious when you begin to compare.

CHAPTER TWENTY-ONE
TROUBLE SHOOTING

Trouble shooting the diesel engine is a real pleasure. It is a very simple engine and it can be handled with a modicum of effort. Many of the problems with the diesel engine are in the product of setup rather than any mechanical difficulty. We will try to discuss the salient features of both mechanical and setup problems.

Begin with the things the diesel requires in order to run. It must have air, fuel, and sufficient compression, each at the right time. If the engine does not start, one of these things is missing. If the engine starts and runs but has other problems, those problems will still be related in one way or another to the lack of one or more of the above.

Let us examine a few of the specific problems which the diesel encounters on a more or less regular basis and I will suggest a probable cure for each of them.

1. THE ENGINE FAILS TO START: Suppose the diesel does fail to start. Where do I begin to look? Does the engine rotate at a good speed on the starter motor? No? Check the battery. The battery is good? If no, recharge or replace the battery. If yes, continue the checks.

Turn the switch key and check for current at the starter solenoid. Do you have current here?

If, no, check the ignition switch. If, yes, continue the checks. Can you hear the solenoid engage with a strong click when the key is turned to the start position? If, no, the solenoid is faulty. If, yes, continue the checks.

If each of these parts is operating effectively and the engine does not turn over, it is probably frozen.

2. THE ENGINE TURNS RAPIDLY ON THE STARTER, YET FAILS TO RUN: Let us begin with the fuel supply. You will need a bit of help for this one. Turn the engine over with the starter. As it rotates, go to an injector, take a wrench and crack (slightly loosen) the fuel delivery line.

Did you get a good discharge of fuel? Repeat the process at each injector, individually.

There cannot be any bubbles in this discharge. If you see bubbles in the line you must continue to operate the starter until the bubbles disappear. You are seeing the evidence of an air lock.

NOTE: Never run the starter motor for more than thirty seconds at one time. Allow the motor to cool for two minutes before the next thirty second operating period.

3. BUBBLES CONTINUE TO APPEAR IN THE LINES: There is a problem with the fuel supply. Work your way backward to the fuel tank. Begin with the high-pressure injector pump. Check the shut down solenoid to be certain it is opening. If, no, repair or replace. If, yes, the injector pump must be bled just as the injectors themselves are bled. Try to remove the air from the injector pump.

If you are able to do so, you must then repeat the bleeding process at each of the injectors. If you cannot remove the air from the injector pump, begin moving backwards towards the fuel tank. Direct injectors and electronic injectors may have a specific bleeding process of their own and one that is different from that we have outlined. Consult your service manual for this procedure but that first step is still to bleed the injection system, if bubbles are present. Beyond the bleeding process, the next steps we will outline are common to all systems.

4. THE FUEL SYSTEM WILL NOT BLEED: Check the low pressure, fuel supply pump and be certain it is operating. Check all fuel line and be certain there are no leaks. Check the fuel filters to be certain they are clean. Check the

gasket on the fuel filters. Look for air leaks at any connection and at the tanks.

Be certain the bayonet pickup in the fuel tank is in place and operational. I have seen a mechanic try for two days to eliminate the leaks in a fuel system that had lost the fuel pick up in the tank. Think about every part of the fuel supply system, eliminate all leaks and then rebleed the system.

5. THERE IS PLENTY OF AIR, THE FUEL SUPPLY IS GOOD, THE ENGINE ROTATES RAPIDLY ON THE STARTER: The engine will almost surely run. If it fails to do so at this point, there is no compression or insufficient compression to start the engine. You probably cannot do anything about this unless there is a true emergency involved.

Starting fluid, sprayed into the engines intake system may cause the engine to start. It can also crack a valve or do other damage to the engine. Use starting fluid only if you must and then only according to the factory directions.

6. THE ENGINE RUNS BUT IT HAS SMOKE IN THE EXHAUST: Here you must be careful because older diesels tend to smoke at least a bit. The question of whether or not that smoke is a problem varies from engine to engine. An experienced mechanic can tell you if the smoke is excessive.

7. THE SMOKE IS GRAY: This is usually a sign that the diesel is using or burning some oil. The oil control rings are the likely culprits. If your oil control rings have failed the engine will need some type of overhaul.

8. THE SMOKE IS BLACK: The problem here is usually excessive or unburned fuel. Unfortunately, there are several reasons why the engine may have this black smoke in the exhaust. A restricted air intake, bad or poor fuel, or a stuck injector will all cause this phenomenon. Restricted airflow to the engine room will require instruments to check.

A visual inspection will suffice for the air filter. A sample to the laboratory will do for the fuel check.

You can check the injectors with an easy procedure. How is this done? With the engine running at operating temperature and at low to moderate speeds, crack the injector lines, one at a time. If the injector is bad, the smoke will clear a bit as the engine stops running on that particular cylinder. Be certain to tighten the injector lines again after each test and before moving on to the next injector. Keep a rag handy to catch the spilled fuel.

If none of these above possibilities proves to be the culprit, the engine may have internal problems. Worn rings or leaky valves will reduce the compression and cause the engine to smoke. A compression test is a good start.

9. THE COMPRESSION TEST CAN SHOW SEVERAL THINGS:

a. The compression is even on all cylinders but it is below minimum factory specifications. In this situation you probably have faulty compression rings. This can be further confirmed by a leak down test. If the engine fails the leak down test, it must be overhauled.

b. The engine has low compression on two adjacent cylinders but the remaining cylinders are at an acceptable level. In this situation the cylinder head gasket has usually blown out between the cylinders. You will have to replace the head gasket.

c. The compression is erratic on all the cylinders and in some cylinders, below factory minimum. In this case you are probably losing the valves. A valve regrind is likely indicated.

Oddly enough, a majority of the problems, which arise with diesel engines, are located in the above paragraphs. Not included are the major internal components of the engine such as pistons, connecting rods, crankshafts, and bearings. These are truly major components and any failure of one or all of them require a complete tear down.

The other problem has to do with setup of the engine/drive train. The engine must have exhaust hoses big enough to let it breathe freely. It must be able to turn the propeller with which it is equipped to full factory recommended RPMs.

The propeller that is too large for the engine will cause

it to smoke and that is the least of the problems it can cause. In extreme cases it may destroy your engine. Excessive fuel consumption and a loss of horsepower are other problems associated with improper propellers.

There is nothing described above which cannot be approached by any person with reasonable mechanical skills, excepting piston ring or valve failure. These you will recognize but be unable to repair.

The heart of trouble shooting is diagnosis. Almost any mechanic is competent to repair your engine if he can first find the problem. If the mechanic is struggling in an effort to repair your engine, the most likely problem he faces is an improper diagnosis.

Remember each of the things you have learned about the engine in this book. See every part as it moves and get the sequence of events firmly embedded in your mind. Remember those things the engine requires in order to run and look for those which are missing.

Do these things and you will become an extraordinary troubleshooter for within these principles lie the alpha and omega of engine performance. There is one further item I would recommend and that is a complete service manual.

This book will tell you why the engine works and give you the insight that enables you to find problems within a category. The service manual will give you specific instructions about your particular engine. Exact clearances, tolerances, and specifications are provided in the service manual.

Special procedures to accomplish those things described in this book are found in the service manual. DO NOT TRY TO REMEMBER THE NUMBERS. Always consult the manual, even if you just saw the very item yesterday. Do not trust your memory when an engine worth thousands of dollars is at stake.

The more engines you build, the less, not more, you should try to remember. The service manual does not forget. Use it.

CHAPTER TWENTY-TWO
AUXILIARY ENGINES

This chapter will concern itself with auxiliary engines for sailboats; more particularly those sailboats under 35 feet and those auxiliary engines of 65 horsepower and below. Engines within this group are worthy of note for several reasons, most of which have to do with maintenance.

The design, principles of construction, and trouble shooting of the auxiliary engine is essentially the same as for any other diesel but these smaller engines operate in a very unhappy situation. In a word, they are out of sight and out of mind. Maintenance on the auxiliary engine is often sketchy or nonexistent.

This lackadaisical approach to engine care is a terrible mistake and few auxiliary engines have very many hours on the clock when they have to come down for maintenance. There are other reasons for this as well, one is situational. Besides being out of sight in the stern of the vessel, that auxiliary is also below the water line.

This requires special mufflers and lift systems. It also calls for special hoses and fittings. Each of these is a potential leak and each is going to require attention at some time. Then we have the matter of intermittent operation. These engines are often off line for days or even weeks at a time. Suddenly they are expected to start without pause, then perform flawlessly. Few engines can manage this easily and some not at all.

What should the sail boater do about this? I recommend several things. Start with a visual inspection. Every

30 days you should look through the engine compartment and check for rust or corrosion. Whether the offending part is electrical, mechanical, or hydraulic, if it is rusted or corroded, fix it. Water fittings, exhaust manifolds, or other metal parts should be cleaned with a wire brush, osphoed, and painted.

Badly rusted or corroded parts and cracked or broken hoses should be replaced at this time. Check the rubber belt drives to alternator and water pump. Inspect the crankcase for possible leaks at seals or pan. Corroded electrical connections should be replaced and they should be installed with soldered joints, using resin cored solder, not acid core.

Figure 22
Courtesy of Yanmar

Auxiliary 56 hp diesel.

The auxiliary engine is truly below the water line and sometimes by as much as a foot or two. Any leaks in the exhaust system are likely to enter the engine. For this reason premature failure is all too common in sailboat engines. Moisture also attacks the internal parts.

The auxiliary engine often runs for short times and never quite gets up to temperature. Docking and like chores may only keep the engine in operation for a short time. The engine is often asked to pull while it is still cold and then shut down before it has an opportunity to evaporate the moisture out of its depths.

For this reason the auxiliary often loses valves at an early age. Rust builds up on the seats and faces of the valves, destroys the seal and the result is low compression. The engine will be harder to start and it will not run very well.

There are other problems caused by his intermittent operation. A cold engine can make a lot of exhaust residue. Over a period of time this residue can almost clog or completely clog the exhaust lines and/or the exhaust elbow. I have had sailboat auxiliaries in my shop with exhaust lines that were so clogged with gunk a screwdriver or chisel and hammer were required to clear them. These engines were in the last stages of complete failure to start or run. The available power was down to a small fraction of the potential, yet the owner did nothing about it. So long as that engine would make one more berthing or one more trip out of the marina, it had served its purpose.

There is a rather ridiculous line of reasoning that suggests, "We don't need the silly things most of the time anyway." There are a few purists who do not employ an auxiliary engine, do not even have one in the vessel, but they are few and far between. Are you really one of these?

You may think so until that day when the wind begins to blow, hard. With bare poles and a reef or shore in sight is a poor time to discover that the auxiliary which you have failed for so many days is now going to fail you.

Auxiliaries should be run at every one of those thirty-day inspections, at a minimum. They should be run until the temperature gauge comes up to full operating temperature and remains there for several minutes.

The starting batteries for auxiliaries must be serviced. Almost any sailboat has a house battery, a generator, or both. Thus the starting battery may be subject to the same treatment as the engine itself and totally forgotten about until needed. Starting batteries for the auxiliary should also be inspected periodically for connections, electrolyte level, and state of charge.

Controls for the auxiliary are very important. They should be disassembled and greased at all wear points during your annual inspection. Cable ends need a coating of grease at those periodic inspections. Just wipe off the old grease and add a bit of new.

I like clutch oil and engine oil pressure gauges. I also like low-pressure warnings and shutdown protection on both assemblies. Always check the clutch oil on the auxiliary at the same time that you check engine oil and coolant and before starting the engine.

I change clutch oil at every change of the engine oil but you should consult your owner's manual about this. The manufacturer may specify changes for the clutch oil at greater or lesser intervals than the engine oil. Always observe the manufacturers recommendations.

Particular attention should be paid to lubricants and their recommended change intervals. The change periods may be given in chronological intervals as well as operating time intervals. The instructions may read, "Change every 100 hours of operation or every 6 months, whichever comes first." This is most important. The detergent package in the lubricant has antioxidants and anticorrosion elements that are only effective for limited times. It is the chemical inhibitors that protect your engine internally and will only do so for a limited interval.

Some transmissions will free wheel without a problem and some will not. Freewheeling occurs when the vessel is under sail alone and the propeller is driving the propeller shaft.

This should not happen if the vessel is equipped with a feathering propeller or a shaft binder.

If your vessel does not have a feathering propeller here is a word of caution. It MAY be equipped with a transmission, which will not successfully free wheel. In the instance where the manufacturer is aware of this situation, the vessel will usually have some type of mechanism on the propeller shaft to bind or freeze the shaft during those times when the engine is off line.

This mechanism is very important and you should maintain it as you do the remainder of the power train. If the shaft binder fails and if the transmission is not designed to free wheel, serious damage will occur to the bearings and internal parts of the transmission.

There is not a great deal of effort involved here. This binder will either work or it will not. The shaft will freeze or it will continue to turn when you are underway. If no binder is present the vessel likely does not need one but if one is affixed to the shaft it should be kept in good working order.

Water pumps on the auxiliary are asked to accept a greater load than those on a conventional engine. Because the engine is below the water line, the pumps are faced with an added backpressure. For this reason the impellers, seals, and gaskets should be kept in excellent working order.

Many of the auxiliary diesel engines have water pumps installed as standard equipment, which are only marginally sufficient at best. They provide adequate pressure during the early life of the impeller when it is working at its greatest efficiency. Before the pump is very old they may not provide enough cooling water. The rubber blades actually drag the case of the pump at low speeds. The pump provides positive displacement operation at this time and it can pump against a pretty fair head pressure. Once the blades begin to wear this effect is lost.

An impeller that is satisfactory in ordinary service may actually be worn out under the extended loads of underwater use. Always keep a close check on the flow of cooling water and on the temperature of the exhaust parts attached to any auxiliary.

Whether the engine is installed in a sailboat or some other type of vessel, always consult the owner's manual and observe all of the directives contained therein. Your engine will last longer and give better service.

CHAPTER TWENTY-THREE
ENGINE SELECTION

Engine selection is a murky subject and I am not going to give absolute answers. I am going to touch on those general principles that govern the choices you make. Several things dictate the parameters for engine selection. The vessel size, design, and its intended purpose are the basic indicators.

Cost of the engine, cost of operation, period or interval of operation, and safety are secondary factors but very important, nonetheless. There are some installations that are, at least in my mind, the exclusive province of the diesel engine. There are some installations in which the light, high-speed diesel seeks to replace gasoline and may successfully do so.

There are others that are the province of the gasoline engine. The manufacturers of those lighter and faster diesels might well argue the point but I feel they would be reaching for a market that belongs elsewhere.

We discussed some of these comparisons in the chapter on Gasoline versus Diesel. I am going to expand upon that a bit and then explore more carefully those areas in which there is real controversy or a closer possibility for comparison.

Down to specifics. Begin with the sailboat auxiliary. This category is the exclusive province of the diesel engine. The engine is buried down inside a closed environment and gasoline offers an unacceptable hazard in that tight engine compartment.

The auxiliary may have to run for many hours and draw on a very limited fuel supply in doing so. Dependability, even under highly adverse conditions, is an absolute requirement for the sailboat engine and so I select diesel engines for this purpose.

High-speed sport fishermen of 38 feet or greater length are the provinces of the diesel engine. These vessels need engines with 400 horsepower or more available at cruising speed. There simply are no gasoline engines available today that can provide this amount of horsepower and survive the daily grind of doing so.

Commercial vessels from 35 feet in length, up to the largest such vessels you may encounter are best served by the diesel engine. The dependability and economy it can provide are very important here. This category goes to the diesel engine, exclusively.

Trawlers with displacement hulls, particularly those intended for long range operation are also best suited for diesel engines. The engine location and fire hazard on this vessel is not quite so great as that on a sailboat auxiliary but it is still very real.

The larger yachts, those of 40 feet and more, are another category that will best utilize diesel power. Below forty feet, this category begins to blur. How fast do you want to go? How many hours do you operate the vessel each year?

Vessels in the forty feet and under group that are constructed on displacement hulls or semi-displacement hulls are not a certain decision. The average owner operates these vessels for 200 hours per year or less. There will be those who dispute this and who in fact do operate their vessels for many more hours annually. This very real division gives validity to the assumption the diesel/gas engine decision can and should be made on multiple input. For this category, I declare a tie.

There are gasoline engines available from Merc Cruiser, Crusader, and others that are available with 250 horsepower and upward. These gasoline engines are much lighter than a diesel engine of comparable horsepower. They are much less expensive to purchase and equipped with Electronic Fuel Injection they are very fuel-efficient. These engines are much quieter than a diesel and it will take many years of fuel savings to equal the difference in fuel consumption.

If you are operating a yacht in the 35 foot to 40 foot range that normally runs at hull speed and operates for only limited hours each year, you will be hard pressed to justify the cost of a diesel. As the hull design begins to reach semi-displacement speeds, 12 miles per hour to 14 miles per hour, that 35 foot to 40-foot hull becomes a question mark.

Here there are still gasoline powered, fuel injected engines that can compete, if the engine hours are 200 or less per year. This category is probably a toss up. Time of operation is a major consideration. The fuel savings will mount up during longer periods of operation. Check your engine log and see if you are exceeding that 200-hour annual barrier. If the answer is, yes, you are a candidate for diesel power. If the answer is, no, you can sort of toss the proverbial coin. What if I intend to run at higher speeds with a full planing hull? There is no argument now. Go diesel. This advice will extend upward from the 40 foot sizes, throughout the range. Large yacht, go diesel.

I cannot expand this treatise to cover every possible category of engine/vessel installation but there is one group I am particularly interested in. That group of vessels is the 26-foot fishing vessels, whether center console designs or small cabin cruisers. In this category the weight of an engine is important, due to the limited planing surface available in 26 feet of boat. This category is best served with a gasoline engine. The reasons that I am going to give you are from my heart as well as my head. Some may charge that they are more subjective than objective but I will have to risk it.

Here goes:

The small boat is a living, breathing animal that has a life and character of its own. The operator should need few days aboard to become familiar with most of its moods and idiosyncrasies. These smaller vessels are very sensitive to loading, both in amount and distribution.

Many of them are capable of incredible performance in

relation to their size and displacement and they can handle extremely adverse weather conditions. All of these assertions are based upon the assumption that the vessel is well found, properly loaded, and has a sufficient amount of readily available power.

At my home in Pensacola, Florida, there is a pass into the sea. At the mouth of that pass is a shallow bar that reaches outwards towards the open Gulf. Even the slightest onshore wind will pile up breakers on that bar and when the wind reaches 15 knots there are plenty of six footers.

The really good boats are those we can put sideways into those breakers and expect them to come out on the other side. Roll it up on the full curl of the surf. Run down the wave, just below the crest and feel the hull beneath your feet. Listen to the engine and take the pulse of that machine on which you may someday bet your life.

For more than 50 years I have gone to the deeper reaches of the Gulf, in small boats. For my purposes I want a gasoline powered engine and I have always used one to do this. The power to weight ratio is outstanding. A good gasoline engine develops much greater torque figures than the average person believes. With the proper gearing and a good propeller, the 26-foot and under vessel will accelerate instantly, upon demand. With seas at the stern it will float lightly and respond well. With seas on the bow it will rise, as needed, all so long as the weight is within reason for the hull design.

I do not care for a vessel/engine package in which the engines cost very nearly half the total cost of the entire package. I do not believe that the turbo diesel engine, which is able to match a 250 horsepower gasoline unit for performance, will be nearly as light or nearly as quiet as the gasoline engine.

I further believe that if both units are used for the same speeds, the diesel engine is unlikely to ever justify its cost. Every man has his own opinion and every man must make decisions based upon that belief. For me, the fishing boat in the 26 foot and under category should be powered with a gasoline engine. There is another 26 foot and under vessel I believe should be diesel powered. That is the life boat or dory hull. These vessels are also capable of incredible performance under very difficult conditions. They have 6-knot speeds and 15 horsepower is probably adequate, 20 horsepower is surely sufficient.

This hull will never outrun bad news or offer a speedy flight from approaching weather. What it will do is to match the most capable skipper in sheer determination to survive. The diesel engine is the only selection for this category of vessel and weight is not important since the limited horsepower means limited size.

When a five hundred-foot tanker sinks, that 28-foot lifeboat was for many years the only salvation of the capable skipper. He simply had to make do with limited engine size and a large dose of seamanship. Award this vessel category to the diesel engine.

FINAL THOUGHTS

I hope you have enjoyed this book as much as I have enjoyed writing it. If you ever have the opportunity, take a tour through one of the old World War II Liberty Ships and look at the oil screws. These engines drove the Liberty Ships into and out of harm's way.

They may seem primitive to your eyes but they were the power that seamen depended upon when the Wolf Packs prowled. Try to get a tour through an old diesel submarine and look at the engines that powered the Silent Fleet. These are old engines but they tell a story of their own.

If you are really interested in the history of diesel and if you get the opportunity to travel the continent you can find all manner of old and unusual engines in the fishing boats and commercial vessels of Germany and Scandinavia. Even smaller boats in the twenty-foot class may still have very old engines installed.

The engine is revered in those less fortunate areas of the world where the throwaway mentality has not yet penetrated. Many fishermen will go to extreme lengths to preserve that old power plant and with that kind of dedication, the diesel engine may last a man for his entire lifetime. The lore of diesel is as fascinating as any story you can imagine and it is certainly worth pursuing when you are near any seaport.

Practical Seamanship
Written By David S. Yetman

Captain Jack's Basic Navigation
Written By Jack I. Davis

Creating Comfort Afloat
Written By Janet Groene

Living Aboard
Written By Janet Groene

Racing The Ice To Cape Horn
Written By Frank Guernsey & Cy Zoerner

Marine Weather Forecasting
Written By J. Frank Brumbaugh

Complete Guide To Gasoline Marine Engines
Written By John Fleming

Complete Guide To Outboard Engines
Written By John Fleming

Complete Guide To Diesel Marine Engines
Written By John Fleming

Trouble Shooting Gasoline Marine Engines
Written By John Fleming

Trailer Boats
Written By Alex Zidock

Skipper's Handbook
Written By Robert S. Grossman

White Squall
The Last Voyage Of Albatross
Written By Richard E. Langford

Cruising South
What to Expect Along The ICW
Written By Joan Healy

Electronics Aboard
Written By Stephen Fishman

Five Against The Sea
A True Story of Courage & Survival
Written By Ron Arias

Scuttlebutt
Seafaring History & Lore
Written By Captain John Guest USCG Ret.

Cruising The South Pacific
Written By Douglas Austin

Catch of The Day
How To Catch, Clean & Cook It
Written By Carla Johnson

VHF Marine Radio Handbook
Written By Mike Whitehead

REVIEWS

Mark Klossner - Mercury Marine
Dealer Training Manager, Mercury University

"Bravo to John Fleming for translating the technical jargon of marine propulsion in a way that's easy for everyone to understand. His three books, *Complete Guide To Outboard Engines, Complete Guide To Gasoline Marine Engines,* and *Complete Guide To Diesel Marine Engines* are well-written, thoughtfully laid out and very informative. They should be required reading for anyone who owns, fixes or sells marine engines!"

Jerry Renninger - Southern Boating

If you own a marine diesel engine, you owe it to yourself to read this book. At the very least you'll come away better equipped to communicate with your mechanic.

Pete McDonald - Boating

If you want to better understand the big iron toiling under the deck of you sportfish, pick up a copy of the *Complete Guide To Diesel Marine Engines* by John Fleming. The book takes you through the ins and outs of diesel power in terms even a landlubber could understand. It explains the hows and whys of diesel engines, but there's also a chapter on the basics of troubleshooting and another on selecting the right engine for your boat. For the die-hard, there's even a chapter on the mathematics of diesels. If you want a solid understanding of how a diesel operates, this is one hands-on guide to bring aboard.

ABOUT THE AUTHOR

John Fleming

John Fleming has conducted a 60 year love affair with engines and never met one he did not like. There have been a few that were so exciting he remembers them like an old flame but they all serve a purpose and they are all a part of my memories.

The first engine he built was a 1948 model, 4.2 horsepower, Champion outboard engine. He was 9 years old which made it monumental task. To see and hold the parts his father had described was fascinating.

He held a United States Coast Guard, 500 ton masters ticket and has a total of more than 3,000 days at sea.

John has run boats of many types and varieties in 44 States and 3 countries: crossed the Okefenokee in an airboat and canoe, ran the Everglades from Flamingo Park to Chokloskee Island and from Whitewater Bay to the head of the Little Shark River.

For eight years he held a State of Florida Teachers Certificate to teach engine repair in the State.

John and his wife have run delivery charters across the Gulf of Mexico from Brownsville, Texas to Key West, Florida and up the Atlantic Seaboard as far as Barnegat Bay. They have owned vessels which they have operated for dive charters, fishing charters and towing services.

He has written more than 3,500 articles for magazines and newspapers.

DATE DUE

GAYLORD			PRINTED IN U.S.A.

Printed in the United States
40342LVS00002B/132

9 781892 216243